DESIGNER
KNIT HOME

**24 Room-by-Room
Coordinated Knits**
to Create a Look
You'll Love to Live In

ERIN BLACK

**STACKPOLE
BOOKS**
Guilford, Connecticut

Published by Stackpole Books
An imprint of The Rowman & Littlefield Publishing Group, Inc.
4501 Forbes Blvd., Ste. 200
Lanham, MD 20706
www.stackpolebooks.com

Distributed by NATIONAL BOOK NETWORK
800-462-6420

Photography by Erin Black

We have made every effort to ensure the accuracy and completeness of these instructions. We cannot, however, be responsible for human error, typographical mistakes, or variations in individual work.

British Library Cataloguing in Publication Information available

Library of Congress Cataloging-in-Publication Data

Names: Black, Erin, 1980- author.
Title: Designer knit home : 24 room-by-room coordinated knits to create a
   look you'll love to live in / Erin Black.
Description: Guilford, Connecticut : Stackpole Books, [2019]
Identifiers: LCCN 2018033970 (print) | LCCN 2018035894 (ebook) | ISBN
   9780811768184 | ISBN 9780811719711 (paperback) | ISBN 9780811768184
   (ebook)
Subjects: LCSH: Knitting—Patterns. | House furnishings.
Classification: LCC TT825 (ebook) | LCC TT825 .B6284 2019 (print) | DDC
   746.43/2—dc23
LC record available at https://lccn.loc.gov/2018033970

♾™ The paper used in this publication meets the minimum requirements of American National Standard for Information Sciences—Permanence of Paper for Printed Library Materials, ANSI/NISO Z39.48-1992.

Printed in the United States of America

Contents

Introduction   vi

Living Room

Cable Stripes Throw Blanket   2

Triple Cable Lapghan   6

Twisted Cable Cushion   10

Cable Knit Footstool   13

Garden

Dandelion Throw   18

Honeycomb Cushion   22

Terrarium Sling   25

Master Bedroom

Pinstripe Blanket   30

Herringbone Throw Blanket   33

Linen Stitch Pillowcase   36

Guest Bedroom

Diamond Lace Blanket   40

Daisy Pillowcase   44

Eyelet Throw Blanket   47

Cozy Slipper Socks   50

Office

Simple Stockinette
   Cocoon Blanket   54

Simple Stockinette Cushion   57

Simple Stockinette Basket Bag   60

Kid's Room

Chevron Blanket 66

Panda Throw Blanket 69

Double Stuffed Polka
   Dot Pillowcase 72

Stripy Ball Cover 75

Nursery

Hexagon Throw Blanket 80

Triangle Baby Blanket 86

Textural Lovie 90

Stitches and Techniques **94**

Abbreviations 118

Knitting Needle Sizes
   for this Book 119

Yarn Weight Chart for this Book 120

Yarn Sources 121

Introduction

The trend of creating oversize knits using thick and lofty yarn seems to be one that has no intention of fading, and I, for one, couldn't be happier that chunky knits are here to stay! Who doesn't love large, gorgeous, cozy projects that work up fast?

When I first started writing patterns for Midknits, I absolutely adored the chunky knits I was seeing all over Pinterest, but trying to track down the super bulky yarns (or affording them) was tricky. Also I had heard horror stories of trying to care for constantly shedding bulky yarns and couldn't imagine the nightmare of making an incredibly luxurious blanket and having it covered in toddler jam-hands (have you ever noticed that their hands are always sticky?). I just couldn't justify spending the money on the glorious bulky yarn when I knew the odds that it would survive my household were minimal. But I still like to have nice things, and I was sure other people out there were in the same situation, so I decided to design a chunky cable-knit blanket that would use multiple strands of an easily accessible and economical worsted-weight acrylic yarn.

The blanket was a success! It turned out just as I had imagined (if not even a little better), and it was machine washable and dryable, didn't take long to knit, and didn't cost a fortune in supplies. It also became a super popular pattern on my website and, after five years, is still the most knitted project in my library. I couldn't think of a better way to celebrate this pattern than by creating an entire book filled with chunky knit blanket patterns! As an homage to my first pattern, you will find some chunky cable-knit designs in the Living Room section on page 1 of this book. But I didn't stop with cables! This book includes an array of other chunky knitting techniques such as lace, stockinette, chevrons, stripes, and more!

While I was writing the patterns for *Designer Knit Home*, I got a chance to play with many multiple strands of yarn and have discovered some other great benefits besides being less expensive and more durable than some jumbo yarns. Because you can purchase worsted-weight yarns pretty much everywhere, and you can find them in a huge array of colors, you aren't limited to what you can find in the jumbo yarn section. You also can create incredible textures while using multiple strands. Although I am partial to the smooth texture you get when you use a bunch of the same yarn together, you can easily create your own variegated yarns, in whatever colors you choose, simply by using different colored strands together. (Find this technique used in the Herringbone Throw Blanket pattern on page 33.)

I have loved writing this book for you and have thoroughly enjoyed creating each and every pattern. Part of what I loved so much was getting to play with the many strands of yarn, and I would encourage you to do the same. Use these patterns as a jumping-off point for your own creativity and try knitting them in different fibers, colors, and textures, bringing together a mix of different strands to make your own unique yarns. I can't wait to see all of your yarn-y projects, so don't forget to tag @Midknits #MidknitsMakers on Instagram, Facebook, and Pinterest!

Happy knitting,

MIDKNITS

www.Midknits.com

LIVING
ROOM

Cable Stripes Throw Blanket

You must stripe it! Creating vertically striped colorwork with multiple strands of yarn looks tricky, but this join-as-you-go striped blanket allows you to work with one color at a time so you won't have to fuss with switching back and forth while you work the cables. This technique also makes it easy to add width to your blanket, so you can adjust the size of this cozy throw to suit your needs.

FINISHED SIZE
42 x 54 in (107 x 137 cm), without tassels

SKILL LEVEL
Intermediate

YARN
Bernat Softee Chunky; #6 super bulky-weight yarn; 100% acrylic; 108 yd (99 m), 3.5 oz (100 g) per skein; machine wash and dry
- **A:** 12 skeins #28008 Natural
- **B:** 14 skeins #28219 Seagreen (12 for blanket and 2 for tassels)

NEEDLES
Size US 50 (25.0 mm) circular needle, 24 in (61 cm) long, or size to obtain gauge

NOTIONS
Tapestry needle
Cable needle (jumbo)
Stitch markers (minimum 10)

GAUGE
4 sts x 6 rows in stockinette stitch with four strands held tog = 4 in (10 cm) square

SPECIAL TECHNIQUES
Join-as-you-knit vertical stripes on page 112
Tassels on page 116

Pattern

Each panel will be worked from the bottom up on the RS of your work and will be joined to the RH side of the preceding panel using the join-as-you-knit vertical stripe technique.

Panel 1

With four strands of **A** held tog, CO 5 sts.
Row 1 (RS): Sl 1 st pwise, purl all sts to end of row.
Row 2: Knit all sts to end of row.
Rows 3–84: Rep rows 1–2.
BO all sts.

Panel 2

With four strands of **B** held tog, CO 6 sts.
Rows 1, 3, and 5 (RS): Sl first st kwise, knit all sts to last st, sl last st kwise; sl RH needle through front leg of first st of corresponding row on previous panel, place LH needle through front of first two sts on RH needle, knit both sts tog.
Rows 2, 4, 6, and 8: Purl all sts to end of row.
Row 7: Sl 3 sts to cn in back, sl 1 st kwise from LH needle (mark with a stitch marker so it is easier to

find the 7th row edge stitch when attaching the next panel), k2 from LH needle, k2 from cn, sl last st from cn kwise; sl RH needle through front leg of first st of corresponding row on previous panel, place LH needle through front of first two sts on RH needle, knit both sts tog.
Rows 9–80: Rep rows 1–8 nine more times.
Rows 81 and 83: Rep row 1.
Rows 82 and 84: Rep row 2.
BO all sts.

Panel 3

With four strands of **A** held tog, CO 5 sts.
Row 1 (RS): Sl 1 st pwise, purl all sts to last st, sl last st pwise; sl RH needle through back leg of first st of corresponding row on previous panel, place LH needle through back of first two sts on RH needle, purl both stitches tog.
Row 2: Knit all sts to end of row.
Rows 3–84: Rep rows 1–2.
BO all sts.

Rep Panels 2 and 3 four more times. On the final rep of Panel 3, purl the first st of each RS row, instead of slipping it, to achieve a finished edge.
Weave in loose ends.

Finishing

Using yarn **B**, make ten 9 in (23 cm) tassels for both ends of each cable stripe.
Tie each tassel to one end of a stripe by weaving one 14 in (36 cm) strand of yarn **B** through the top of the tassel and through the end of the stripe, securing with a knot. Trim and weave in loose ends.

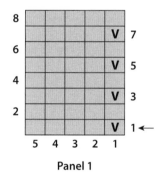

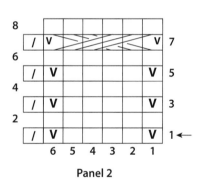

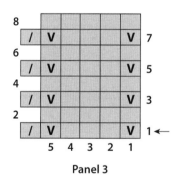

Panel 1

Panel 2

Panel 3

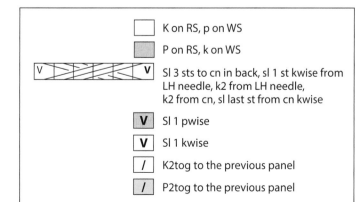

	K on RS, p on WS
	P on RS, k on WS
V — V	Sl 3 sts to cn in back, sl 1 st kwise from LH needle, k2 from LH needle, k2 from cn, sl last st from cn kwise
V	Sl 1 pwise
V	Sl 1 kwise
/	K2tog to the previous panel
/	P2tog to the previous panel

Triple Cable Lapghan

Three times a charm! This lapgan is the perfect size to keep your legs warm without a lot of extra bulk, ensuring that you won't overheat when you cuddle up underneath it. Perfect for rocking-chair cuddling or baby bundling, this charming, cute, and cozy lapghan really is a triple treat.

FINISHED SIZE
39 x 39 in (99 x 99 cm)

SKILL LEVEL
Intermediate

YARN
Patons Classic Wool Worsted; #4 medium-weight yarn;
100% wool; 210 yd (192 m), 3.5 oz (100 g) per skein;
hand wash and dry flat
- 13 skeins #00202 Aran

You will need to divide the final skein evenly into 6 center-pull bobbins/balls.

NEEDLES
Size US 36 (20.0 mm) circular needle, 36 in (91 cm) long,
or size to obtain gauge

NOTIONS
Tapestry needle
Cable needle (jumbo)

GAUGE
5 sts x 7 rows in stockinette stitch with six strands held
tog = 4 in (10 cm) square

SPECIAL TECHNIQUES
Cables on page 105

SPECIAL ABBREVIATIONS
C6B (cable six back): Sl the next 3 sts to cn and hold in
    back of work, k3 from LH needle, k3 from cn.
C6F (cable six front): Sl the next 3 sts to cn and hold in
    front of work, k3 from LH needle, k3 from cn.

Pattern

With six strands held tog, CO 57 sts.

Rows 1–10: *K1, p1, rep from * to last st, k1.

Rows 11, 13, and 15: (K1, p1) three times, k3, p3, *k9, p3, rep from * to last 9 sts, k3, (p1, k1) three times.

Row 12 and all even-numbered rows: (K1, p1) three times, k1, p2, k3, *p9, k3, rep from * to last 9 sts, p2, k1, (p1, k1) three times.

Row 17: (K1, p1) three times, k3, p3, *k3, C6B, p3, rep from * to last 9 sts, k3, (p1, k1) three times.

Row 19: (K1, p1) three times, k3, p3, *k9, p3, rep from * to last 9 sts, k3, (p1, k1) three times.

Row 21: (K1, p1) three times, k3, p3, *C6F, k3, p3, rep from * to last 9 sts, k3, (p1, k1) three times.

Row 23: (K1, p1) three times, k3, p3, *k9, p3, rep from * to last 9 sts, k3, (p1, k1) three times.

Row 25: (K1, p1) three times, k3, p3, *k3, C6B, p3, rep from * to last 9 sts, k3, (p1, k1) three times.

Row 27: (K1, p1) three times, k3, p3, *k9, p3, rep from * to last 9 sts, k3, (p1, k1) three times.

Row 29: (K1, p1) three times, k3, p3, *C6F, k3, p3, rep from * to last 9 sts, k3, (p1, k1) three times.

Rows 31, 33, 35, 37, 39, and 41: (K1, p1) three times, k3, p3, *k9, p3, rep from * to last 9 sts, k3, (p1, k1) three times.

Rows 43–66: Rep rows 13 through 36 one more time.

Rows 67–76: *K1, p1, rep from * to last st, k1.

BO all sts. Weave in loose ends.

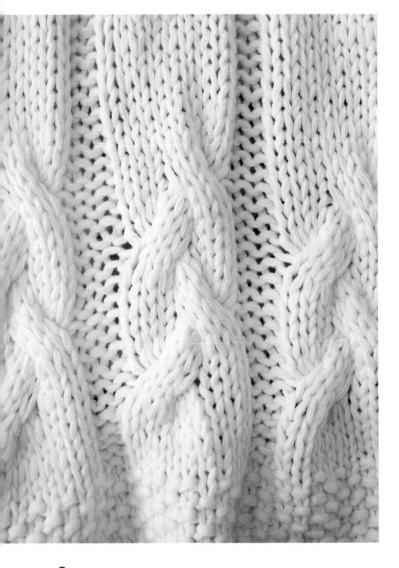

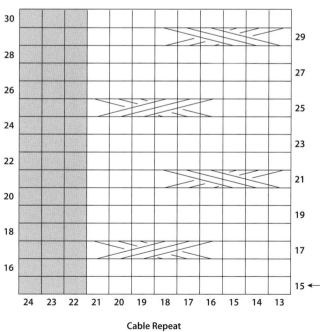

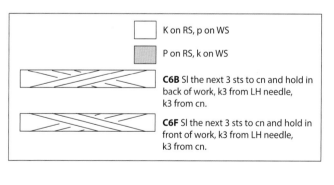

	K on RS, p on WS
	P on RS, k on WS
	C6B Sl the next 3 sts to cn and hold in back of work, k3 from LH needle, k3 from cn.
	C6F Sl the next 3 sts to cn and hold in front of work, k3 from LH needle, k3 from cn.

Cable Repeat

Twisted Cable Cushion

Warm, cozy, and gorgeous! This large throw cushion is the perfect combination of style and functionality, complete with zipper for easy maintenance. Big enough for two heads, this is the perfect cushion for curling up for a movie-watching sofa cuddle.

FINISHED SIZE
27 x 27 in (69 x 69 cm)
Preassembled size is 21 x 48 in (53 x 122 cm).

SKILL LEVEL
Intermediate

YARN
Patons Classic Wool Worsted; #4 medium-weight yarn;
100% wool; 210 yd (192 m), 3.5 oz (100 g) per skein;
hand wash and dry flat
• 9 skeins #00202 Aran

NEEDLES
Size US 36 (20.0 mm) circular needle, 24 in (61 cm) long,
or size to obtain gauge

NOTIONS
Tapestry needle
Cable needle (jumbo)
26 in (66 cm) square pillow form
24 in (61 cm) zipper to match yarn

GAUGE
5 sts x 7 rows in stockinette stitch with six strands held
tog = 4 in (10 cm) square

SPECIAL TECHNIQUES
Cables on page 105
Mattress stitch on page 107
Zippers on page 112

SPECIAL ABBREVIATIONS
C6B (cable six back): Sl the next 3 sts to cn and hold in
   back of work, k3 from LH needle, k3 from cn.
C6F (cable six front): Sl the next 3 sts to cn and hold in
   front of work, k3 from LH needle, k3 from cn.

Pattern

With six strands held tog, CO 33 sts.

Row 1: K6, p2, k2, p2, k9, p2, k2, p2, k6.

Row 2 and all even-numbered rows: P6, k2, p2, k2, p9, k2, p2, k2, p6.

Row 3: K6, p2, k2, p2, k3, C6B, p2, k2, p2, k6.

Row 5: Rep row 1.

Row 7: K6, p2, k2, p2, C6F, k3, p2, k2, p2, k6.

Rows 9–96: Rep rows 1–8 eleven more times.

BO all sts. Weave in loose ends.

Finishing

Fold the pillow cover in half, WS to WS, aligning the CO and BO edges. Seam the two side seams together using mattress stitch.

Seam together the CO and BO edges, installing a zipper in the center of the seam.

Weave in loose ends.

Stuff the cover with your pillow form.

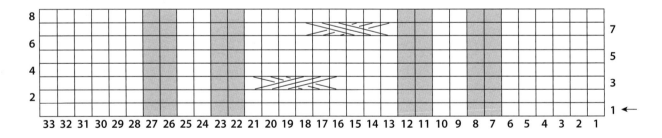

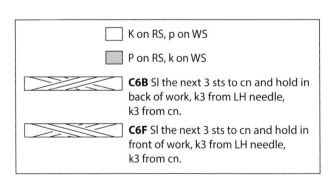

☐ K on RS, p on WS

▨ P on RS, k on WS

C6B Sl the next 3 sts to cn and hold in back of work, k3 from LH needle, k3 from cn.

C6F Sl the next 3 sts to cn and hold in front of work, k3 from LH needle, k3 from cn.

Cable Knit Footstool

Feet, seat, knit! This footstool makes a great place to put your feet up and relax, or an extra seat to lounge on. Durable cotton/nylon yarn is cable knit together to form a sturdy cover that can easily be taken off the beanbag for washing, making this footstool easy to care for.

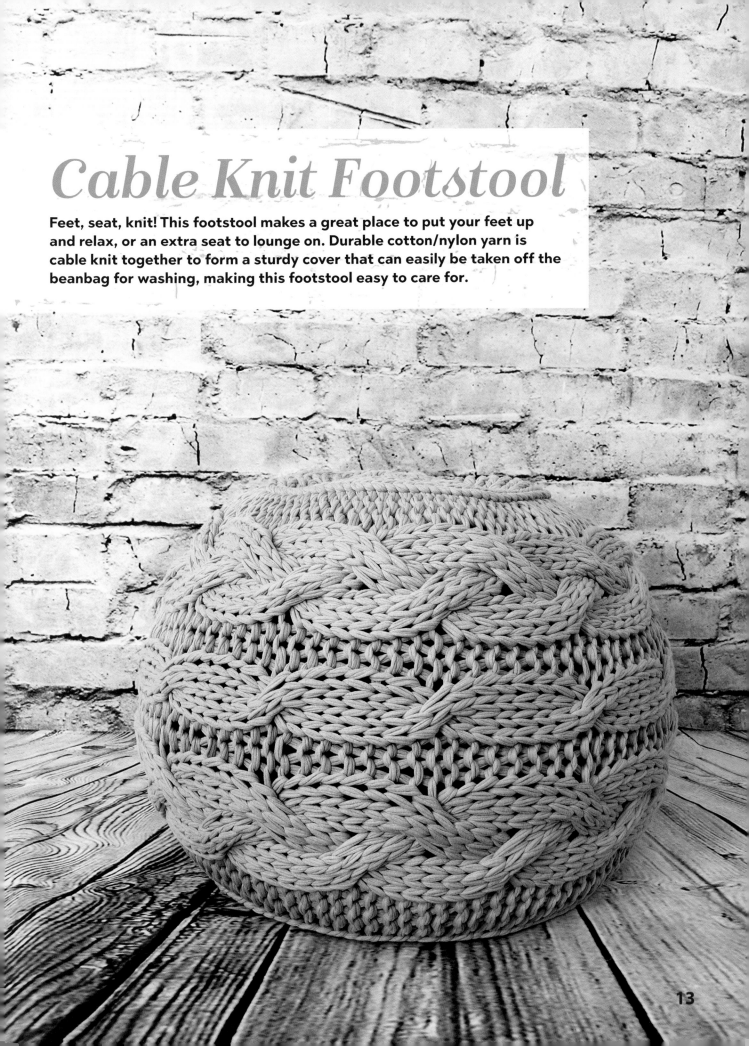

FINISHED SIZE

25 in (64 cm) diameter x 18 in (46 cm) tall
Preassembled size is 26 x 42 in (66 x 107 cm).

SKILL LEVEL

Intermediate

YARN

Bernat Maker Home Dec; #5 bulky-weight yarn; 72% cotton, 28% nylon; 317 yd (290 m), 8.8 oz (250 g) per skein; machine wash and dry
- 8 skeins #11008 Clay

You will need to divide the final 2 skeins evenly into 6 center-pull bobbins/balls.

NEEDLES

Size US 36 (20.0 mm) circular needle, 24 in (61 cm) long, or size to obtain gauge

NOTIONS

Large-eye tapestry needle
Cable needle (jumbo)
Cord lock toggle
24 in (61 cm) diameter drum-shaped beanbag chair

GAUGE

5 sts x 9 rows in stockinette stitch with six strands held tog = 4 in (10 cm) square

SPECIAL TECHNIQUES

Cables on page 105
Invisible horizontal seam on page 108

SPECIAL ABBREVIATIONS

C4F (cable four front): Sl the next 2 sts to cn and hold in front of work, k2 from LH needle, k2 from cn.
C6B (cable six back): Sl the next 3 sts to cn and hold in back of work, k3 from LH needle, k3 from cn.
C6F (cable six front): Sl the next 3 sts to cn and hold in front of work, k3 from LH needle, k3 from cn.

Pattern

With six strands held tog, CO 44 sts.

Row 1: K6, p3, k9, p2, k4, p2, k9, p3, k6.

Row 2 and all even-numbered rows: P6, k3, p9, k2, p4, k2, p9, k3, p6.

Row 3: K6, p3, k3, C6B, p2, C4F, p2, C6F, k3, p3, k6.

Row 5: Rep row 1.

Row 7: K6, p3, C6F, k3, p2, k4, p2, k3, C6B, p3, k6.

Rows 9–96: Rep rows 1–8 eleven more times.

BO all sts. Weave in loose ends.

Finishing

Align the CO and BO edges and seam them together using six strands held tog as one and the invisible horizontal seam technique to form a tube.

Cut three strands of yarn 70 in (178 cm) long and hold together as one. With tapestry needle, weave into every third stitch along one open end of the tube. Pull the yarn taut to cinch the top of the tube and close the opening as much as possible. Tie off the yarn and weave in the loose ends. You may need to cut three more strands and repeat the weaving and cinching technique a second time, weaving the yarn into every third stitch between the stitches you have already cinched, to fully close the opening.

Cut three strands of yarn 70 in (178 cm) long and hold together as one strand. With tapestry needle, weave into every third stitch along the remaining open edge of the tube. Secure the two yarn ends together with the toggle lock and then knot the yarn so the toggle won't fall off.

Stuff the cover with the filled beanbag chair. Cinch the cover tightly with the strands from the previous step and secure with the toggle. Stuff the yarn ends into the footstool and flip it over, toggle side down, to use.

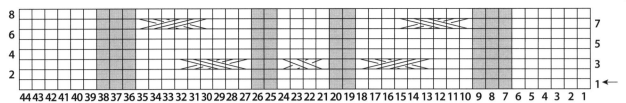

Work rows 1–8 twelve times.

☐ K on RS, p on WS

▨ P on RS, k on WS

C4F Sl the next 2 sts to cn and hold in front of work, k2 from LH needle, k2 from cn.

C6B Sl the next 3 sts to cn and hold in back of work, k3 from LH needle, k3 from cn.

C6F Sl the next 3 sts to cn and hold in front of work, k3 from LH needle, k3 from cn.

GARDEN

Dandelion Throw

Tiptoe through the . . . dandelions! The luxurious sheen of silk and bamboo is paired with a delicate and whimsical dandelion stitch to create this gorgeous throw. Laid effortlessly across a lap or elegantly around your shoulders, this blanket is the perfect accessory to keep off a summer evening chill.

FINISHED SIZE
40 x 40 in (102 x 102 cm)

SKILL LEVEL
Intermediate

YARN
Patons Silk Bamboo; #3 light-weight yarn; 70% viscose from bamboo, 30% silk; 102 yd (93 m), 2.2 oz (65 g) per skein; hand wash and dry flat
- 17 skeins #85046 Stone

You will need to divide the final 2 skeins evenly into 6 center-pull bobbins.

NEEDLES
Size US 15 (10.0 mm) circular needle, 36 in (91 cm) long, or size to obtain gauge

NOTIONS
Tapestry needle

GAUGE
9 sts x 14 rows in pattern stitch with three strands held tog = 4 in (10 cm) square

SPECIAL STITCHES
Dandelion: [Insert RH needle through front of third st down from the second st on LH needle (this is the space you will use to make all the loops of your dandelion), pull up a loop onto the RH needle, k2 from LH needle] 3 times.

Pattern

With three strands of yarn held tog, CO 91 sts.

Rows 1–6: K1, *p1, k1, rep from * to end of row.

Row 7: K1, (p1, k1) twice, knit to last 5 sts, (k1, p1) twice, k1.

Row 8: K1, (p1, k1) twice, purl to last 5 sts, (k1, p1) twice, k1.

Row 9: Rep row 7.

Row 10: Rep row 8.

Row 11: K1, (p1, k1) twice, k3, Dandelion, *k2, Dandelion, rep from * to last 5 sts, (k1, p1) twice, k1.

Row 12: K1, (p1, k1) twice, *p2, (p2tog, p1) three times, rep from * to last 6 sts, p1, (k1, p1) twice, k1.

Rows 13–16: Rep rows 7–10.

Row 17: K1, (p1, k1) twice, k7, *Dandelion, k2, rep from * to last 9 sts, k4, (k1, p1) twice, k1.

Row 18: K1, (p1, k1) twice, p4, *p2, (p2tog, p1) 3 times, rep from * to last 10 sts, p5, (k1, p1) twice, k1.

Rows 19–126: Rep rows 7–18.

Rows 127–134: Rep rows 7–14.

Rows 135–140: K1, *p1, k1, rep from * to end of row.

BO all sts. Weave in loose ends.

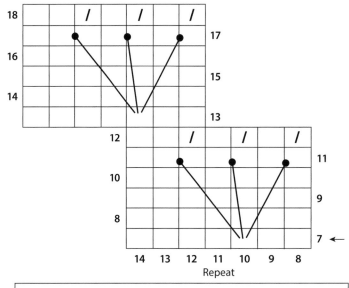

Repeat

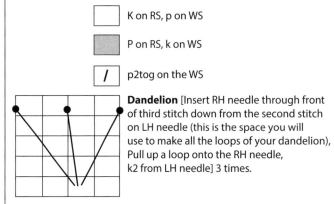

K on RS, p on WS

P on RS, k on WS

/ p2tog on the WS

Dandelion [Insert RH needle through front of third stitch down from the second stitch on LH needle (this is the space you will use to make all the loops of your dandelion), Pull up a loop onto the RH needle, k2 from LH needle] 3 times.

Honeycomb Cushion

The bee's knees! Soft wool knit with a whimsical cable stitch makes this gorgeous lumbar cushion a textural masterpiece. The addition of a contrasting zipper and tassel modernize this sweet pillow cover and make it easy to care for.

FINISHED SIZE

12 x 18 in (30 x 46 cm)
Preassembled size is 17 x 24 in (43 x 61 cm).

SKILL LEVEL

Intermediate

YARN

A: Patons Classic Wool Worsted; #4 medium-weight yarn; 100% wool; 210 yd (192 m), 3.5 oz (100 g) per skein; hand wash and dry flat
• 5 skeins #00202 Aran
You will need to divide the final 2 skeins evenly into 3 center-pull bobbins.

B: Patons Silk Bamboo; #3 light-weight yarn; 70% viscose from bamboo, 30% silk; 102 yd (93 m), 2.2 oz (65 g) per skein; hand wash and dry flat
• 1 skein #85046 Stone (for tassel)

NEEDLES

Size US 15 (10.0 mm) circular needle, 24 in (61 cm) long, or size to obtain gauge
US N/P (10.0 mm) crochet hook (for seaming)

NOTIONS

Tapestry needle
Cable needle
12 x 18 in (30 x 46 cm) pillow form
16 in (41 cm) zipper

GAUGE

13½ sts x 14½ rows in pattern with three strands held tog = 4 in (10 cm) square

SPECIAL TECHNIQUES

Cables on page 105
Crochet slip stitch together on page 108
Zippers on page 112
Tassels on page 116

SPECIAL ABBREVIATIONS

C4B (cable four back): Sl 2 sts pwise to cn and hold at back of work, k2 from LH needle, k2 from cn.
C4F (cable four front): Sl the next 2 sts to cn and hold in front of work, k2 from LH needle, k2 from cn.

Pattern

With three strands of **A** held tog, CO 58 sts.
Row 1: K1, *C4F, C4B, rep from * to last st, k1.
Row 2 and all even-numbered rows: Purl all sts.
Row 3: Knit all sts.
Row 5: K1, *C4B, C4F, rep from * to last st, k1.
Row 7: Knit all sts.
Rows 9–80: Rep rows 1–8 nine more times.
Rows 81–87: Rep rows 1–7.
BO all sts in purl. Weave in loose ends.

Finishing

Fold the pillow cover in half, RS to RS, aligning the CO
   and BO edges. Seam one short side and the long
   sides together using the crochet slip stitch together
   method and **A**.
Turn the cover right-side out.
Seam together the final short side, installing a zipper in
   the center of the seam.
Weave in loose ends.
With **B**, make and attach a tassel to the zipper pull.
Stuff the cover with your pillow form.

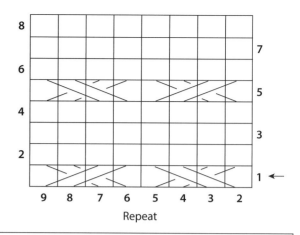

Repeat

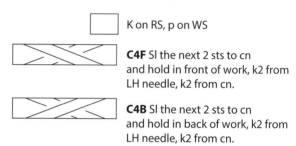

	K on RS, p on WS
	C4F Sl the next 2 sts to cn and hold in front of work, k2 from LH needle, k2 from cn.
	C4B Sl the next 2 sts to cn and hold in back of work, k2 from LH needle, k2 from cn.

Terrarium Sling

Sling into action! Cotton and needles come together to create this beautiful terrarium sling. Knit in simple stockinette stitch, this sling will hold a bowl or round terrarium and showcase the gorgeous greenery inside.

FINISHED SIZE
16 in (41 cm) tall with 8 in (20 cm) diameter pocket

SKILL LEVEL
Intermediate

YARN
Lily Sugar'n Cream; #4 medium-weight yarn; 100% cotton; 120 yd (109 m), 2.5 oz (71 g) per skein; machine wash and dry
- 1 skein #00042 Tea Rose or #00004 Ecru

NEEDLES
Size US 19 (15.0 mm) circular needles, 36 in (91 cm) long, or size to obtain gauge

NOTIONS
Tapestry needle
1½ in (4 cm) wooden hanging ring
6–11 in (15–28 cm) diameter bowl

GAUGE
8 sts x 8 rows in stockinette stitch with two strands held tog = 4 in (10 cm) square

SPECIAL TECHNIQUES
Magic loop knitting in the round on page 101
Tassels on page 116

Pattern

With two strands held tog, CO 6 sts. Join and work in the rnd using the magic loop method.

Rnd 1: Kfb all sts to end of rnd. (12 sts)
Rnd 2: *K1, kfb, rep from * to end of rnd. (18 sts)
Rnd 3: Knit all sts.
Rnd 4: *K2, kfb, rep from * to end of rnd. (24 sts)
Rnd 5: Knit all sts.
Rnd 6: *K3, kfb, rep from * to end of rnd. (30 sts)
Rnd 7: Knit all sts.

Work back and forth over the next 10 sts to make one strap.

Rows 8, 10, 12, and 14: Knit all sts. (10 sts)
Rows 9, 11, 13, and 15: Purl all sts.
Row 16: K1, k2tog, k4, k2tog, k1. (8 sts)
Rows 17, 19, and 21: Purl all sts.
Rows 18 and 20: Knit all sts.
Row 22: K1, k2tog, k2, k2tog, k1. (6 sts)
Row 23: Purl all sts.
Row 24: Knit all sts
Row 25: Purl all sts.

Break yarn. Leave the 10 live working sts on a stitch holder.

Rejoin yarn to work rows 8 through 25 on the next 10-st section, and then again on the final 10-st section.

Place all 18 sts (A, B, and C from diagram) back on the needles, in order, being sure not to twist them.

Begin working in the rnd.

Rnds 26–29: Knit all sts.

Break yarn, leaving a 12 in (30 cm) tail. To bind off, use your tapestry needle to weave the tail through all the live sts on your needle. Pull the tail tight to cinch the top of your terrarium sling together and tie off the tail. Weave in loose ends.

Finishing

Attach ring to top of sling by sewing through the top of the sling and around the bottom of the ring. Secure in place with a knot and weave in loose ends. Place the bowl in the bottom part of the sling and adjust to make sure it is secure before hanging.

Add tassel to bottom if desired.

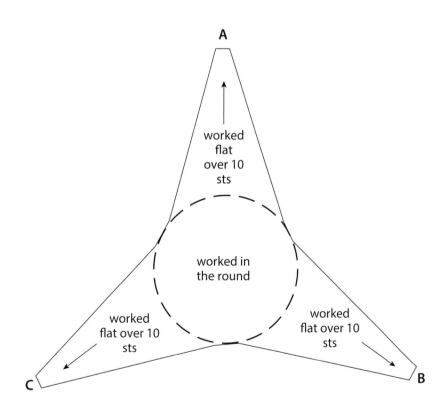

MASTER
BEDROOM

Pinstripe Blanket

Suit up with this gorgeous, sophisticated blanket perfect to dress up any bed. The oversize stitches and lofty yarn make this blanket quick and cozy to work up. The fact that it is knit in simple stockinette stitch, with the stripes added to the surface as a finishing detail, means that this blanket is deceptively easy to create! Don't forget to add that extra oomph with gigantic tassels for the perfect finishing touch.

FINISHED SIZES

Twin: 70 x 90 in (178 x 229 cm)
Double: 85 x 90 in (216 x 229 cm)
Queen: 85 x 100 in (216 x 254 cm)
King: 100 x 100 in (254 x 254 cm)
Throughout the pattern, the sizes/instructions are given as Twin (Double, Queen, King).

SKILL LEVEL

Easy

YARN

Bernat Softee Chunky; #6 super bulky-weight yarn; 100% acrylic; 108 yd (99 m), 3.5 oz (100 g) per skein; machine wash and dry
- **A:** 36 (44, 49, 58) skeins #28008 Natural
- **B:** 4 (5, 6, 7) skeins #28040 Black

Bernat Roving; #5 bulky-weight yarn; 80% acrylic, 20% wool; 120 yd (109 m), 3.5 oz (100 g) per skein; hand wash and dry flat
- **C:** 4 (5, 5, 6) skeins #00033 Flint, for tassels

NEEDLES

Size US 50 (25.0 mm) circular needle, 60 in (152 cm) long, or size to obtain gauge
Size US 50 (25.0 mm) crochet hook, for pinstripes

NOTIONS

Tapestry needle

GAUGE

4 sts x 5 rows in stockinette stitch with four strands held tog = 4 in (10 cm) square

SPECIAL TECHNIQUES

Surface slip stitch on page 113
Tassels on page 116

Pattern

Instructions given for Twin (Double, Queen, King).

With four strands of **A** held tog, CO 65 (76, 76, 87) sts.

Row 1 (RS): Knit all sts.

Row 2: Purl all sts.

Rep rows 1–2 until blanket measures 90 in (229 cm) for Twin and Double or 100 in (254 cm) for Queen and King.

BO all sts. Weave in loose ends.

Pinstripes

With **B** and crochet hook, surface slip stitch pinstripes on the RS of the blanket working in each stitch in a column from the CO edge to the BO edge, in every 11th column of stockinette V stitches.

Finishing

With **C**, make 10 (12, 12, 14) 9 in (23 cm) long tassels for both ends of each black surface slip-stitch stripe.

Tie each tassel to one end of a stripe by weaving one 14 in (35.5 cm) strand of yarn **B** through the top of the tassel and through the end of the stripe. Secure by tying a tight bow that will keep the tassel secure but will allow it to be removed before washing the blanket. Repeat this step for each tassel.

Herringbone Throw Blanket

Men's suiting on point! The gorgeous herringbone stitch is used to create a sophisticated throw that will keep you warm and cozy. Although the pattern is traditional in nature, the oversize stitches and variegation created with the use of different colored strands of yarn modernize this classic textile.

FINISHED SIZE
42 x 52 in (107 x 132 cm)

SKILL LEVEL
Intermediate

YARN
Patons Canadiana; #4 medium-weight yarn; 100% acrylic; 205 yd (187 m), 3.5 oz (100 g) per skein; machine wash and dry
- **A:** 10 skeins #10042 Dark Grey Mix
- **B:** 2 skeins #10008 Aran

NEEDLES
Size US 19 (15.0 mm) circular needle, 36 in (91 cm) long, or size to obtain gauge

NOTIONS
Tapestry needle

GAUGE
13 sts x 9 rows in pattern stitch with two strands held tog = 4 in (10 cm) square

SPECIAL ABBREVIATIONS
K2tog tbl (knit two together through the back loops): Insert your RH needle through the back loop of 2 sts pwise, knit both sts tog.

Pattern

With two strands of **A** held tog, CO 140 sts.

Row 1 (RS): *K2tog tbl dropping only the first st off the needle, rep from * to last st, k1.

Row 2: *P2tog dropping only the first st off the needle, rep from * to last st, p1.

Rows 3–56: Rep rows 1–2.

Break one strand of yarn **A** and attach yarn **B** so that you are now working with two strands of yarn together, one of yarn **A** and one of yarn **B**.

Rows 57–96: Rep rows 1–2.

Break strand of yarn **B** and attach new strand of yarn **A** so that you are now working with two strands of yarn **A** together.

Rows 97–118: Rep rows 1–2.

BO all sts. Weave in loose ends.

2   人
人   1 ←
1
Repeat

| | 人 | K2tog tbl dropping only the first st off the needle on the RS |
| | 人 | P2tog dropping only the first st off the needle on the WS |

Linen Stitch Pillowcase

Textural textiles! This linen stitch pillowcase will add warmth and sophistication to your space. Although knit, the textile resembles a textural weave that has a timeless elegance. Add a fancy looped fringe to modernize this pillowcase for the perfect accent for any bedroom.

FINISHED SIZE

20 x 30 in (51 x 76 cm) stuffed pillow
Pre-stuffed size is 19 x 29 in (48 x 74 cm).

SKILL LEVEL

Intermediate

YARN

A: Patons Canadiana; #4 medium-weight yarn; 100% acrylic; 205 yd (187 m), 3.5 oz (100 g) per skein; machine wash and dry
• 7 skeins #10008 Aran
B: Bernat Roving; #5 bulky-weight yarn; 80% acrylic, 20% wool; 120 yd (109 m), 3.5 oz (100 g) per skein; hand wash and dry flat
• 1 skein #00100 Rice Paper, for trim

NEEDLES

Size US 19 (15.0 mm) circular needle, 24 in (61 cm) long, or size to obtain gauge
US N/P (10.0 mm) crochet hook, for seaming

NOTIONS

Tapestry needle
18 in (46 cm) zipper
Queen size pillow: 20 x 30 in (51 x 76 cm)

GAUGE

10 sts x 17 rows in pattern stitch with three strands of **A** held tog = 4 in (10 cm) square

SPECIAL TECHNIQUES

Crochet slip stitch together on page 108
Zippers on page 112
Loop fringe on page 117

Pattern (Make 2)

With three strands of **A** held tog, CO 70 sts.

Row 1 (RS): K1, *K1, move yarn to front, sl next st pwise, move yarn to back, rep from * to last st, k1.

Row 2: P1, *p1, move yarn to back, sl next st pwise, move yarn to front, rep from * to last st, p1.

Rows 3–80: Rep rows 1–2.

BO all sts. Weave in loose ends.

Finishing

Weave in loose ends.

Align the edges of both pieces of the pillowcase, WS to WS, making sure both CO and BO edges are aligned. With three strands of **A**, seam both long sides and one short side together using the crochet slip stitch together seaming method to add a decorative chain to the front of the pillow. Continue in the same manner to add the decorative chain to the front piece only along the final short side.

Seam together the final short side, installing a zipper in the center of the seam.

Weave in loose ends.

With **B**, add loop fringe into the chain created when seaming around the perimeter on the front side of your pillow.

Stuff the cover with your pillow form.

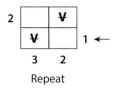

Repeat

	K on RS, p on WS
V	Sl 1 pwise with yarn at RS of work

GUEST
BEDROOM

Diamond Lace Blanket

Diamonds are a girl's best friend! This blanket is the perfect piece to add a playful, lacy accent to a room without getting too frilly. Geometric, with large spaces in the fabric, this piece is perfect as a bedcover over a contrasting backdrop to really bring out the detail.

FINISHED SIZE

Twin: 61 x 90 in (155 x 229 cm)
Double: 84 x 90 in (213 x 229 cm)
Queen: 91½ x 104 in (232 x 264 cm)
King: 107 x 104 in (272 x 264 cm)
Throughout the pattern, the sizes/instructions are given as Twin (Double, Queen, King).

SKILL LEVEL

Advanced

YARN

Bernat Satin; #4 medium-weight yarn; 100% acrylic;
200 yd (183 m), 3.5 oz (100 g) per skein; machine wash and dry

- **A:** 3 (5, 5, 6) skeins #04021 Linen
- **B:** 25 (35, 44, 52) skeins #04232 Sage

You will need to divide the final skein evenly into 3 center-pull bobbins/balls.

NEEDLES

Size US 19 (15.0 mm) circular needle, 60 in (152 cm) long, or size to obtain gauge

NOTIONS

Tapestry needle

GAUGE

9 sts x 10 rows in pattern stitch with three strands of yarn held tog = 4 in (10 cm) square

Pattern

Instructions given for Twin (Double, Queen, King).
Work throughout holding three strands tog as one.
With **A**, CO 129 (177, 193, 225) sts.
Rows 1–22: Knit all sts.
Break yarn.
Join yarn **B**.
Row 23: Knit all sts.
Row 24: K1,*k5, p2, k1, p2, k6, rep from * to end of row.
Row 25: *K5, k2tog, yo, k3, yo, k2tog tbl, k4, rep from * to last st, k1.
Row 26: K1,*k4, p3, k1, p3, k5, rep from * to end of row.
Row 27: *K4, k2tog, yo, k5, yo, k2tog tbl, k3, rep from * to last st, k1.
Row 28: K1,*k3, p4, k1, p4, k4, rep from * to end of row.
Row 29: *K3, k2tog, yo, k7, yo, k2tog tbl, k2, rep from * to last st, k1.
Row 30: K1,*k2, p5, k1, p5, k3, rep from * to end of row.
Row 31: *K2, k2tog, yo, k2, k2tog, yo, k1, yo, k2tog tbl, k2, yo, k2tog tbl, k1, rep from * to last st, k1.
Row 32: K1,*k1, p5, k3, p5, k2, rep from * to end of row.
Row 33: *K1, k2tog, yo, k2, k2tog, yo, k3, yo, k2tog tbl, k2, yo, k2tog tbl, rep from * to last st, k1.
Row 34: K1,*p5, k5, p5, k1, rep from * to end of row.
Row 35: *K4, k2tog, yo, k5, yo, k2tog tbl, k3, rep from * to last st, k1.
Row 36: K1,*p4, k7, p4, k1, rep from * to end of row.
Row 37: *K3, k2tog, yo, k7, yo, k2tog tbl, k2, rep from * to last st, k1.
Row 38: K1,*p3, k9, p3, k1, rep from * to end of row.
Row 39: *K2, k2tog, yo, k9, yo, k2tog tbl, k1, rep from * to last st, k1.
Row 40: K1,*p2, k11, p2, k1, rep from * to end of row.
Row 41: Knit all sts.
Row 42: K1,*p2, k11, p2, k1, rep from * to end of row.
Row 43: *K2, yo, k2tog tbl, k9, k2tog, yo, k1, rep from * to last st, k1.
Row 44: K1,*p3, k9, p3, k1, rep from * to end of row.
Row 45: *K3, yo, k2tog tbl, k7, k2tog, yo, k2, rep from * to last st, k1.
Row 46: K1,*p4, k7, p4, k1, rep from * to end of row.
Row 47: *K4, yo, k2tog tbl, k5, k2tog, yo, k3, rep from * to last st, k1.
Row 48: K1,*p5, k5, p5, k1, rep from * to end of row.
Row 49: *K1, yo, k2tog tbl, k2, yo, k2tog tbl, k3, k2tog, yo, k2, k2tog, yo; rep from * to last st, k1.
Row 50: K1,*k1, p5, k3, p5, k2, rep from * to end of row.
Row 51: *K2, yo, k2tog tbl, k2, yo, k2tog tbl, k1, k2tog, yo, k2, k2tog, yo, k1, rep from * to last st, k1.
Row 52: K1,*k2, p5, k1, p5, k3, rep from * to end of row.
Row 53: *K3, yo, k2tog tbl, k7, k2tog, yo, k2, rep from * to last st, k1.
Row 54: K1,*k3, p4, k1, p4, k4, rep from * to end of row.
Row 55: *K4, yo, k2tog tbl, k5, k2tog, yo, k3, rep from * to last st, k1.
Row 56: K1,*k4, p3, k1, p3, k5, rep from * to end of row.
Row 57: *K5, yo, k2tog tbl, k3, k2tog, yo, k4, rep from * to last st, k1.
Row 58: K1,*k5, p2, k1, p2, k6, rep from * to end of row.
Rows 59–238: Rep rows 23–58 five (five, six, six) more times.

BO all sts. Weave in loose ends.

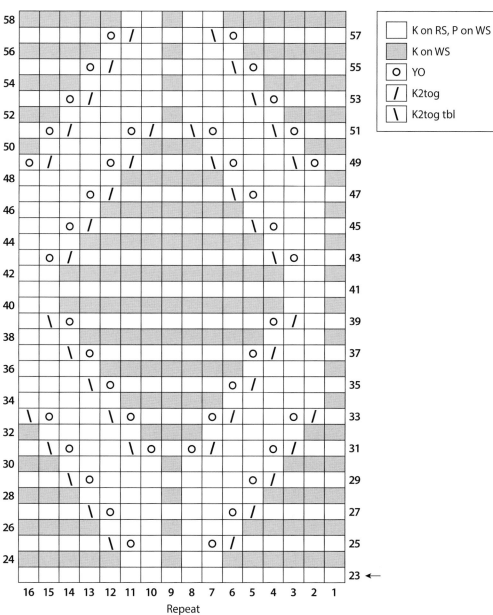

	16	15	14	13	12	11	10	9	8	7	6	5	4	3	2	1	

Repeat

	K on RS, P on WS
▨	K on WS
O	YO
/	K2tog
\	K2tog tbl

Daisy Pillowcase

She loves me, she loves me knot! The gorgeous floral-inspired daisy stitch adds a touch of whimsical texture to this pillowcase. The perfect accent for any bedroom, the repetitive geometric design and the simple lines offer a modern take on textural lace.

FINISHED SIZE

21 x 30 in (53 x 76 cm) stuffed pillow
The preassembled size is 19 x 26 in (48 x 66 cm).

SKILL LEVEL

Intermediate

YARN

Bernat Satin; #4 medium-weight yarn; 100% acrylic;
200 yd (183 m), 3.5 oz (100 g) per skein; machine wash
and dry

• 8 skeins #04232 Sage

*You will need to divide the final 2 skeins evenly into 3
center-pull bobbins/balls.*

NEEDLES

Size US 15 (10.0 mm) circular needle, 30 in (76 cm) long,
or size to obtain gauge
US N/P (10.0 mm) crochet hook, for seaming

NOTIONS

Tapestry needle
Standard 20 x 30 in (51 x 76 cm) bed pillow

GAUGE

11 sts x 14 rows pattern stitch with three strands of yarn
held tog = 4 in (10 cm) square

SPECIAL TECHNIQUES

Crochet slip stitch together on page 108
Zippers on page 112

SPECIAL STITCHES

Daisy: P3tog without dropping the sts off the needle, yo, p3tog again this time dropping the sts off the
needle.

Pattern *(Make 2)*

With three strands held tog, CO 73 sts.

Row 1: Knit all sts.

Row 2: K1, *Daisy, k1, rep from * to end of row.

Row 3: Knit all sts.

Row 4: K1, p1, k1, *Daisy, k1, rep from * to last 2 sts, p1, k1.

Rows 5–68: Rep rows 1–4 sixteen more times.

BO all sts. Weave in loose ends.

Assembly

Align the edges of both pieces of the pillowcase, WS to WS, making sure both CO and BO edges are aligned. With three strands of yarn, seam both long sides and one short side together, using the crochet slip stitch together seaming method, to add a decorative chain to the front of the pillow. Continue in the same manner to add the decorative chain to the front piece along the final short side.

Seam together the final short side, installing a zipper in the center of the seam.

Weave in loose ends.

Stuff the cover with your pillow form.

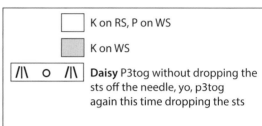

		K on RS, P on WS
		K on WS
/I\ o /I\		**Daisy** P3tog without dropping the sts off the needle, yo, p3tog again this time dropping the sts

Eyelet Throw Blanket

I only have eyes for you! The eyelets in this blanket not only add texture and detail to this cozy throw but also some breathability to a thick and luxurious wool blanket. The sheen on the fringe adds a sparkle and contrasting texture to the loftiness of the wool.

FINISHED SIZE
41 x 52 in (104 x 132 cm)

SKILL LEVEL
Intermediate

YARN
A: Patons Classic Wool Worsted; #4 medium-weight yarn; 100% wool; 210 yd (192 m), 3.5 oz (100 g) per skein; hand wash and dry flat
- 9 skeins #00202 Aran

B: Bernat Satin; #4 medium-weight yarn; 100% acrylic; 200 yd (183 m), 3.5 oz (100 g) per skein; machine wash and dry
- 2 skeins #04021 Linen, for fringe

NEEDLES
Size US 19 (15.0 mm) circular needle, 36 in (91 cm) long, or size to obtain gauge
US N/P (10.0 mm) crochet hook, for attaching fringe

NOTIONS
Tapestry needle

GAUGE
6 sts x 10 rows in pattern stitch with three strands of **A** held tog = 4 in (10 cm) square

SPECIAL TECHNIQUES
Fringe on page 116

Pattern

With three strands of **A** held tog, CO 63 sts.

Row 1: Knit all sts.

Row 2 and all even-numbered rows: Purl all sts.

Row 3: K1, *k1, yo, k2tog, rep from * to last 2 sts, k2.

Row 5: Knit all sts.

Row 7: K1, *k1, ssk, yo, rep from * to last 2 sts, k2.

Rows 9–128: Rep rows 1–8 fifteen more times.

Row 129: Knit all sts.

Row 130: Purl all sts.

BO all sts. Weave in loose ends.

Finishing

Using five 13 in (33. cm) strands of yarn **B** per fringe section, attach fringe in each stitch along both the CO and BO edges of the blanket.

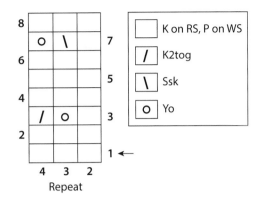

	K on RS, P on WS		
	/	K2tog	
	\	Ssk	
	O	Yo	

Repeat

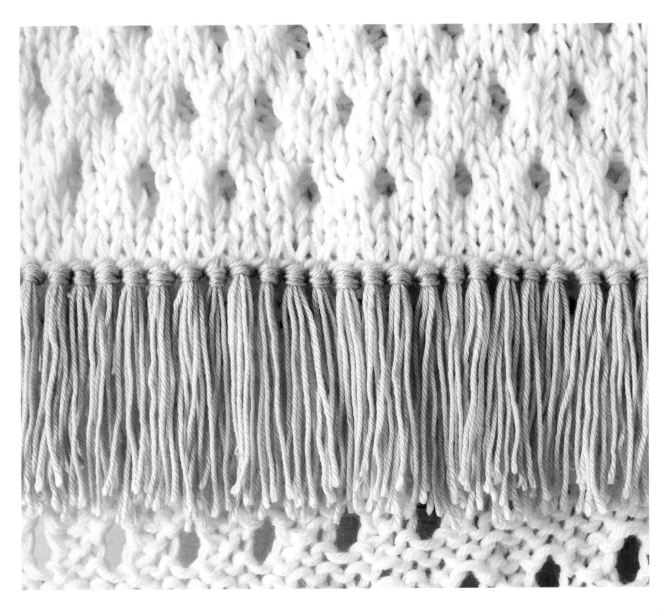

Cozy Slipper Socks

Keep your tootsies toasty! What would make a guest feel more comfortable than a warm pair of stylish slippers? These slipper socks are knit with roving and wool (with added acrylic for ease of care). Knit from the toe up with an afterthought heel, a little shaping, and the tiniest bit of color change, these slippers offer maximum style with minimal effort.

FINISHED SIZE

Small: US sizes 3–6; 6¾ in (17 cm) foot circumference x 8¼ in (21 cm) foot length x 14 in (35.5 cm) high
Medium: US sizes 6–9; 7 in (18 cm) foot circumference x 9 in (23 cm) foot length x 15 in (38 cm) high
Large: US sizes 8–12; 7½ in (19 cm) foot circumference x 10 in (25.5 cm) foot length x 16 in (40.5 cm) high
Sizes throughout are given as Medium (Small, Large).

SKILL LEVEL

Intermediate

YARN

A: Patons Classic Wool Worsted; #4 medium-weight yarn; 100% wool; 210 yd (192 m), 3.5 oz (100 g) per skein; hand wash and dry flat
• 1 skein #77219 Seafoam
B: Bernat Roving; #5 bulky-weight yarn; 80% acrylic, 20% wool; 120 yd (109 m), 3.5 oz (100 g) per skein; hand wash and dry flat
• 2–3 skeins #00100 Rice Paper
Small amount of waste yarn: three strands of a smooth #4 medium-weight yarn held together as one (such as Bernat Satin)

NEEDLES

Size US 15 (10.0 mm) circular needle, 36 in (91 cm) long, or size to obtain gauge

NOTIONS

Tapestry needle

GAUGE

9½ sts x 15 rows in stockinette stitch with 3 strands of **A** or two strands of **B** held tog = 4 in (10 cm) square

SPECIAL TECHNIQUES

Turkish cast-on on page 100
Magic loop on page 101
Kitchener stitch on page 110

SPECIAL ABBREVIATIONS

Ssk (slip, slip, knit): Sl one st kwise to RH needle, sl one stitch pwise to RH needle, place tip of LH needle through front of both slipped sts, k2tog.

Pattern (Make 2)

Instructions given for Medium (Small, Large).

Toe

With three strands of **A** held tog, CO 8 sts using the Turkish CO method. Knit one round to complete the CO.

Continue working in the rnd using the magic loop method, with the stitches split into two groups of 4.

Rnd 1, size Medium only: (K3, kfb) twice. (10 sts)

Rnd 1, size Small only: Knit all sts. (8 sts)

Rnd 1, size Large only: *Kfb, knit to last st on needle, kfb, rep from * to end of rnd. (12 sts)

Rnd 2: *K1, kfb, knit to last 2 sts on needle, kfb, k1, rep from * to end of rnd. (14 [12, 16] sts)

Rnd 3: Knit all sts.

Rnd 4: *K1, kfb, knit to last 2 sts of needle, kfb, k1, rep from * to end of rnd. (18 [16, 20] sts)

Rnd 5: Knit all sts.

Foot

Break yarn and join two strands of **B** held together as one.

Rnds 6–26: Knit all sts until the foot measures approx 5½ in (14 cm) (4½ in [11 cm], 6½ in [17 cm]) long, not including toe.

Rnd 27: Knit the stitches from the first needle. With waste yarn, knit stitches from second needle. Sl the sts you just knit with the waste yarn back to the LH needle (you will return to these stitches to knit the heel later), and continue working the rnd with the original strands of yarn **B** and knit across the stitches of waste yarn to finish the rnd.

Leg

Rnds 28–37: Knit all sts until the leg measures approx 3 in (7.5 cm) (2½ in [6 cm], 3½ in [9 cm]) long, measured from the waste yarn.

Rnd 38: *Knit to last st of needle, kfb, rep from * to end of rnd. (20 [18, 22] sts)

Rnds 39–41: Knit all sts.

Rnd 42: *Kfb, knit to end of needle, rep from * to end of rnd. (22 [20, 24] sts)

Rnds 43–45: Knit all sts.

Rnd 46: *Knit to last st of needle, kfb, rep from * to end of rnd. (24 [22, 26] sts)

Rnds 47–49: Knit all sts.

Rnd 50: *Kfb, knit to end of needle, rep from * to end of rnd. (26 [24, 28] sts)

Rnds 51–53: Knit all sts.

Rnd 54: *Knit to last st of needle, kfb, rep from * to end of rnd. (28 [26, 30] sts)

Rnds 55–57: Knit all sts.

Rnd 58: *Kfb, knit to end of needle, rep from * to end of rnd. (30 [28, 32] sts)

Rnds 59–67: Knit until the leg measures approx 12 in (30 cm) (11½ in [29 cm], 12½ in [32 cm]) long, measured from the waste yarn.

Break yarn. Join three strands of **A**.

Rnds 68–71: *K1, p1, rep from * to end of rnd.

Loosely BO in same ribbed pattern as last rnd.

Break yarn. Weave in loose ends.

Afterthought Heel

Return to waste yarn added in rnd 27.

Remove waste yarn and pick up the live sts from the top of the heel onto first needle and the live sts from the bottom of the heel onto second needle.

With three strands of yarn **A** held together as one and starting at the bottom of the heel (where the heel meets the foot):

Rnd 1: *Pick up and knit one st from foot before first st on first needle, knit across first needle, pick up and knit one st from foot after last stitch on first needle. Rep from * for second needle, picking up and knitting increase sts from leg. (22 [20, 24] sts)

Rnd 2: Knit all sts.

Rnd 3: *K1, ssk, knit to last 3 sts of needle, k2tog, k1, rep from * to end of rnd. (18 [16, 20] sts)

Rnd 4: Knit all sts.

Rnd 5: *K1, ssk, knit to last 3 sts of needle, k2tog, k1, rep from * to end of rnd. (14 [12, 16] sts)

Rnd 6: Knit all sts.

Rnd 7: *K1, ssk, knit to last 3 sts of needle, k2tog, k1, rep from * to end of rnd. (10 [8, 12] sts).

Break yarn, leaving an 18 in (46 cm) long tail.

Use the Kitchener stitch to join the remaining sts from the top of the heel to the remaining sts from the bottom of the heel to close the heel of the sock. Weave in loose ends.

OFFICE

Simple Stockinette Cocoon Blanket

Simple and stylish! This cocoon blanket is knit in simple stockinette stitch with an easy color change that runs diagonally across the piece. But that is the only thing simple about this beauty. The addition of buttons along the edge gives you many options for wear; the stitches are large enough for the buttons to fit through anywhere. You can button this blanket up around your neck, or wear it like a cardigan to form the perfect cocoon to keep you warm while you type away at your computer or read a book.

FINISHED SIZE
46 x 40 in (117 x 102 cm)

SKILL LEVEL
Easy

YARN
Bernat Softee Chunky; #6 super bulky-weight yarn;
100% acrylic; 108 yd (99 m), 3.5 oz (100 g) per skein;
machine wash and dry
- **A:** 3 skeins #28008 Natural
- **B:** 5 skeins #28046 Grey Heather

NEEDLES
Size US 36 (20.0 mm) circular needle, 42 in (107 cm)
long, or size to obtain gauge

NOTIONS
Tapestry needle
Ten 1½ in (4 cm) buttons

GAUGE
5 sts x 7 rows in stockinette stitch with two strands held
tog = 4 in (10 cm) square

Pattern

Work holding two strands together as one.

Note: Be sure to keep yarns hanging to the WS of your work when switching to the new color and twist your yarns at each color change to avoid holes.

With two strands of **A** held tog, CO 56 sts.

Row 1 (RS): Knit all sts.

Row 2: Purl all sts.

Row 3: With **A** k55, with **B** k1.

Row 4: With **B** p2, with **A** p54.

Row 5: With **A** k53, with **B** k3.

Row 6: With **B** p4, with **A** p52.

Row 7: With **A** k51, with **B** k5.

Row 8: With **B** p6, with **A** p50.

Rows 9–57: Continue in the same manner as rows 3–8, alternating knit and purl rows decreasing by one yarn **A** st on each row until only yarn **B** sts remain.

Rows 58–74: With **B** continue knitting RS rows, and purling WS rows.

BO all sts. Weave in loose ends.

Finishing

Sew buttons evenly across half of one short side and evenly across the opposite half of the other short side of the blanket (see drawing).

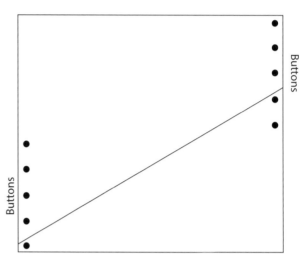

Simple Stockinette Cushion

This is by far the simplest pattern in this book, but it is oh, so cute! This simple stockinette cushion is buttoned up one side using buttons that fit conveniently through the stitches—meaning you don't have to worry about buttonholes. The perfect size to stuff behind your lower back to keep your posture on point, it would also work as a cozy place to rest your head for a mid-morning break.

FINISHED SIZE
14 x 20 in (36 x 51 cm) stuffed pillow
Preassembled size is 18 x 25 in (46 x 63 cm).

SKILL LEVEL
Easy

YARN
Bernat Softee Chunky; #6 super bulky-weight yarn;
100% acrylic; 108 yd (99 m), 3.5 oz (100 g) per skein;
machine wash and dry
- 3 skeins #28008 Natural
*You will need to divide the final skein evenly into 4
center-pull bobbins/balls.*

NEEDLES
Size US 50 (25.0 mm) circular needle, 24 in (61 cm) long,
or size to obtain gauge

NOTIONS
Tapestry needle
Three 2 in (5 cm) buttons
12 x 18 in (30 x 46 cm) pillow form

GAUGE
4 sts x 6 rows in stockinette stitch with four strands of
yarn held tog = 4 in (10 cm) square

SPECIAL TECHNIQUES
Mattress stitch on page 107
Invisible horizontal seam on page 108

Pattern

With four strands of yarn held tog, CO 17 sts.
Row 1 (RS): Knit all sts.
Row 2: Purl all sts.
Rows 3–36: continue alternating knit and purl rows.
BO all sts.

Finishing

Fold the pillow cover in half, WS to WS, aligning the CO and BO edges. Seam one short side using the mattress stitch seaming method and seam the CO and BO edges together using the invisible horizontal seaming method.

Sew three buttons evenly spaced along remaining opening to close.

Weave in loose ends.

Stuff the cover with your pillow form.

Simple Stockinette Basket Bag

Clever container! Knit in the round from the top down, this basket bag is made of simple knit stitches and easy color changes. This basket bag can be a basket by adding a plastic liner to stabilize the sides, a bag by taking out the liner and carrying it around by the handles, and it is reversible (stockinette on one side, reverse stockinette with fringe on the other). That's four possibilities in one project!

FINISHED SIZE
17 in (43 cm) wide x 17 in (43 cm) tall, sitting flat

SKILL LEVEL
Intermediate

YARN
Bernat Maker Home Dec; #5 bulky-weight yarn; 72% cotton, 28% nylon; 317 yd (290 m), 8.8 oz (250 g) per skein; machine wash and dry
- **A:** 2 skeins #11009 Cream
- **B:** 2 skeins #11005 Aqua

NEEDLES
Size US 15 (10.0 mm) circular needle, 36 in (91 cm) long, or size to obtain gauge

NOTIONS
Tapestry needle
Plastic canvas, two pieces 8 in (20 cm) tall x 22 in (56 cm) long

GAUGE
10½ sts x 16 rows in stockinette stitch with two strands of yarn held tog = 4 in (10 cm) square

Pattern

Work with two strands of yarn held tog throughout.

With two strands of **A** held tog, CO 90 sts. Join in the rnd.

Rnds 1–6 (RS): Knit all sts.

Rnd 7: K16, *k1, sl the previous st from the RH needle over this st (as if to bind off), rep from * 14 more times, k30, **k1, sl the previous st from the RH needle over this stitch (as if to bind off), rep from ** 14 more times, k14. (60 sts)

Rnd 8: K15, turn, CO 15 using knitted cast-on method, turn, k30, turn, CO 15 using knitted cast-on method, turn, k15.

Rnds 9–14: Knit all sts.

Note: When cutting yarn for joining, leave an 8 in (20 cm) tail of the old yarn and an 8 in (20 cm) tail of the new yarn hanging to the WS of the work (these tails will form the fringe).

Rnd 15: K44, cut yarn, join yarn **B**, k2, cut yarn, join yarn **A**, k44.

Rnd 16: K43, cut yarn, join yarn **B**, k4, cut yarn, join yarn **A**, k43.

Rnd 17: K42, cut yarn, join yarn **B**, k6, cut yarn, join yarn **A**, k42.

Rnd 18: K41, cut yarn, join yarn **B**, k8, cut yarn, join yarn **A**, k41.

Rnds 19–59: Continue in the same manner as rows 15–18 until only yarn **B** stitches remain.

Rnds 60–64: Knit all sts.

Rnd 65: K1, *k1, sl the previous st from the RH needle over this stitch (as if to bind off), rep from * 8 more times, k27, **k1, sl the previous st from the RH needle over this stitch (as if to bind off), rep from ** 17 more times, k27, ***k1, sl the previous st from the RH needle over this stitch (as if to bind off), rep from *** 7 more times, break yarn and pull through last stitch.

Rejoin yarn **B** to work first group of 27 stitches. You will work back and forth in rows.

Row 66 (RS): Knit all sts.

Row 67: Purl all sts.

Rows 68–77: Repeat rows 66 and 67.

BO all 27 stitches. Break yarn.

Rejoin yarn **B** to work second group of 27 stitches, again working back and forth in rows.

Row 66 (RS): Knit all sts.

Row 67: Purl all sts.

Rows 68–77: Repeat rows 66 and 67.

BO all 27 stitches. Break yarn.

Finishing

FRINGE

Turn the basket inside out. Secure the strands of yarn **A** in place by knotting one strand of yarn to the next along the row of fringe. Be sure to work only with the strands of the same color yarn, and to work each strand in the order it appears starting at the point where yarn **A** and yarn **B** first intersect. As you pull on the yarn ends to tie the knots, be sure to check the stitches on the RS of your work to ensure that your stitches match your gauge. You will work up one side of the basket, and then flip the basket to work up the other side. Repeat for yarn **B**. You now have two layers of fringe along the reverse stockinette side of the basket. Trim the fringe in line with the angle of the colorwork.

SEAMING

Seam the bottom of the basket together. Align the two bottom seam edges and seam together. Align one edge of the bottom side of the basket with the side edge of the base of the basket and seam together (A to B). Repeat for the other side of the basket (C to D). Weave in loose ends.

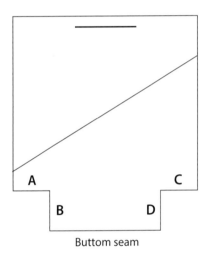

Buttom seam

BASKET STABILIZATION

Overlap one short side of one piece of plastic canvas with one short side of the other piece of the plastic canvas, overlapping the sides by 4 in (10 cm). Seam through the holes along both edges of the overlapping pieces of plastic canvas to secure the pieces together. Wrap the now long piece of plastic canvas into an approximately 36 in (91.5 cm) circumference tube, overlapping the ends by 4 in (10 cm) and seaming to secure in place again. This rigid tube can now be used to support the sides of the basket by placing it inside. It is also removable so that you can use your basket as a bag or turn it inside out to highlight the fringed detail.

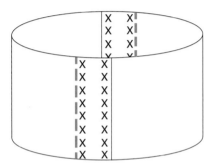

KID'S ROOM

Chevron Blanket

What's black and white and zigzagged all over? This adorable black and white chevron knit blanket is offset by vibrant neon coral pom-poms, making this a fun and playful addition to any kiddo's room. Keeping the pom-poms detachable by simply tying them in place with a bow means they can be removed easily before the blanket is washed, maintaining the easy-to-care-for nature of acrylic.

FINISHED SIZE

Measurements are from valley to tip of chevron.
Twin: 61 x 104 in (155 x 264 cm)
Double: 81 x 104 in (206 x 264 cm)
Queen/King: 101 x 127 in (257 x 323)
Throughout the pattern, the sizes/instructions are given as Twin (Double, Queen/King).

SKILL LEVEL

Easy

YARN

Caron Simply Soft; #4 medium-weight yarn; 100% acrylic; 315 yd (288 m), 6 oz (170 g) per skein; machine wash and dry
- **A:** 14 (19, 29) skeins #9701 White
You will need to divide the final 2 skeins evenly into 6 center-pull bobbins/balls.
- **B:** 12 (16, 25) skeins #9727 Black
- **C:** 4 (6, 7) skeins #9772 Neon Coral, for pom-poms

NEEDLES

Size US 36 (20.0 mm) circular needle, 60 in (152.4 cm) long, or size to obtain gauge

NOTIONS

Tapestry needle

GAUGE

5 sts x 7 rows in stockinette stitch with six strands of yarn held tog = 4 in (10 cm) square
Note: Gauge swatch will not match finished blanket dimensions because of the way the chevron pattern warps the stitches.

SPECIAL TECHNIQUES

Pom-poms on page 115

SPECIAL ABBREVIATIONS

P tbl: Purl through the back loop.

Pattern

Instructions shown for Twin (Double, Queen/King).

Work holding six strands tog as one.

With **A** CO 103 (137, 171) sts.

Row 1: *K1, k2tog, k14, yo, k1, yo, k14, k2tog, rep from * to last st, k1.

Row 2: P1, *p15, p tbl of yo, p1, p tbl of yo, p16, rep from * to end of row.

Rows 3–144: Repeat rows 1–2 for a total of 16 rows in each color alternating yarn **A** and yarn **B**. End after completing 5 (5, 6) yarn **A** sections.

BO all sts. Weave in loose ends.

Finishing

Using yarn **C** make seven (nine, eleven) 6 in (15 cm) diameter pom-poms. Tie each pom-pom to one tip of a chevron section by weaving one 14 in (36 cm) strand of yarn **C** through the center of the pom-pom and through the edge of the blanket. Secure by tying a tight bow that will keep the pom-pom secure but will allow it to be removed before washing the blanket. Repeat this step for each pom-pom.

	K on RS, p on WS
/	K2tog
o	Yo
ℚ	P tbl

Repeat

1 ←

34 33 32 31 30 29 28 27 26 25 24 23 22 21 20 19 18 17 16 15 14 13 12 11 10 9 8 7 6 5 4 3 2 1

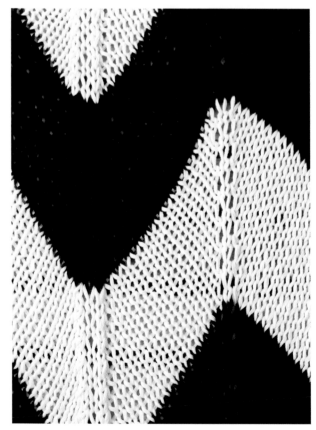

Panda Throw Blanket

What's black and white and cute all over? This panda throw blanket, obviously! The perfect size to cuddle up under, this throw blanket is sure to be a favorite. The duplicate stitch details add an extra element of texture to the blanket, and the tassels add a whimsical touch that any child will enjoy. With a proper rug backing (to keep from slipping), this throw could also make a soft and cushiony bedside rug.

FINISHED SIZE
43 x 56 in (109 x 142 cm)

SKILL LEVEL
Easy

YARN
Caron Simply Soft; #4 medium-weight yarn; 100% acrylic; 315 yd (288 m), 6 oz (170 g) per skein; machine wash and dry
- **A:** 4 skeins #9727 Black
- **B:** 7 skeins #9701 White
- **C:** 1 skein #9739 Soft Green, for tassels

NEEDLES
Size US 36 (20.0 mm) circular needle, 42 in (107 cm) long, or size to obtain gauge

NOTIONS
Tapestry needle

GAUGE
5 sts x 7 rows in stockinette stitch with six strands of yarn held tog = 4 in (10 cm) square

SPECIAL TECHNIQUES
Duplicate stitch on page 114
Tassels on page 116

Pattern

Work holding six strands together as one.

With **A** CO 54 sts.

Row 1 (RS): Knit all sts.

Row 2: Purl all sts.

Rows 3–24: Rep rows 1–2.

Row 25: Repeat Row 1.

Break yarn **A**. Join yarn **B**.

Rows 26–96: Continue working in stockinette stitch as established.

BO all sts. Break yarn. Weave in loose ends.

Finishing

Use six strands of yarn held together as one and the duplicate stitch method to add the bowtie and panda face to the blanket following the color chart. Weave in loose ends.

Using yarn **C** make fourteen 3 in (8 cm) diameter tassels. Tie all fourteen tassels evenly along the bottom edge of the blanket.

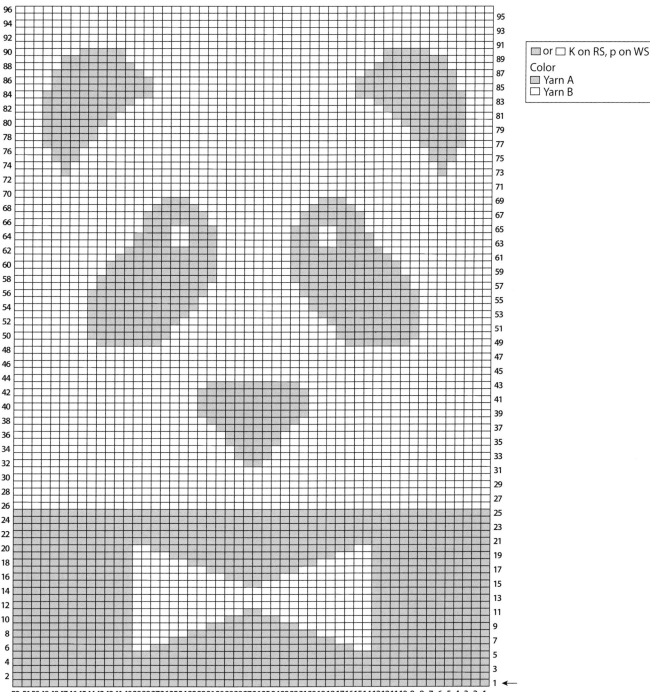

□ or □ K on RS, p on WS
Color
□ Yarn A
□ Yarn B

Double Stuffed
Polka Dot Pillowcase

What's black and white and polka-dotted all over? Oversize bobbles add a wonderful texture to this whimsical, overstuffed pillowcase. With a zippered seam for easy removal and washing, this pillowcase is sure to become a much cuddled and loved piece.

FINISHED SIZE
24 x 32 in (61 x 81 cm) double-stuffed pillow
Preassembled size of each piece is 19 x 28 in (48 x 71 cm).

SKILL LEVEL
Intermediate

YARN
Caron Simply Soft; #4 medium-weight yarn; 100% acrylic; 315 yd (288 m), 6 oz (170 g) per skein; machine wash and dry
- **A:** 4 skeins #9701 White
- **B:** 3 skeins #9727 Black

You will require four strands at ½ yd (0.5 m) each per bobbin per bobble.
- **C:** 1 skein #9739 Soft Green

NEEDLES
Size US 19 (15.0 mm) circular needle, 30 in (76.2 cm) long, or size to obtain gauge
Size US N/P (10.0 mm) crochet hook for seaming

NOTIONS
Tapestry needle
2 queen-size pillows, 20 x 30 in (51 x 76 cm)
18 in (45 cm) zipper

GAUGE
6 sts x 8 rows in stockinette stitch with four strands of yarn held tog = 4 in (10 cm) square

SPECIAL TECHNIQUES
Crochet slip stitch together on page 108
Zippers on page 112

SPECIAL ABBREVIATIONS
Bobble: In same st (k1, yo, k1, yo, k1), turn, purl all 5 sts from bobble, turn, knit all 5 sts from bobble, turn, purl all 5 sts from bobble, turn, k5tog.

Pattern (Make 2)

While working the bobbles, leave the yarn ends hanging to the WS of your work.

Work holding four strands tog as one.

With **A** CO 41 sts.

Row 1 (RS): Knit all sts.

Row 2: Purl all sts.

Row 3: *K2, drop yarn A to WS of work, with **B** make a bobble in next st, with **A** k3, rep from * to end of row.

Row 4: Purl all sts.

Row 5: Knit all sts.

Row 6: Purl all sts.

Row 7: *With **A** k5, with **B** make a bobble in next st, rep from * to last 5 sts, with **A** k5.

Row 8: Purl all sts.

Rows 9–40: Rep rows 1–8 four more times.

Row 41: Knit all sts.

Row 42: Purl all sts.

BO all sts. Break yarn. Knot the strands from each bobble on the WS of the work to secure the stitches in place. Weave in loose ends.

Finishing

Align the edges of both pieces of the pillowcase, WS to WS, making sure both CO and BO edges are aligned. With four strands of yarn **C**, seam both long sides and one short side together using the crochet slip stitch together method to add a decorative chain to the front of the pillow. Continue in the same manner to add the decorative chain to the front piece only along the final short side so that it matches the other three sides.

Using yarn **A**, seam together the final short side, installing a zipper in the center of the seam.

Weave in loose ends.

Stuff the cover with your pillows and close the zipper.

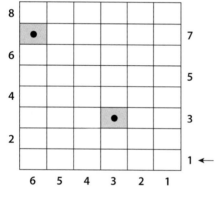

Overall pattern repeat

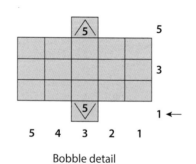

Bobble detail

	K on RS, P on WS
●	**Bobble in same st** (K1, yo, k1, yo, k1), turn, p all 5 sts from bobble, turn, k all 5 sts from bobble, turn, p all 5 sts from bobble, turn, k5tog
\5/	K1, yo, k1, yo, k1
/5\	K5tog
Color	
	Yarn A
	Yarn B

Stripy Ball Cover

What's black and white and striped all over? And bounces? And rolls? This stripy ball, of course! What child wouldn't adore her own oversize ball for epic adventuring? Knit in the round with cotton yarn that has the texture of a cozy T-shirt, this ball cover is easily removable and ready for washing. The textile softens an ordinary exercise ball, and the bottom opening in the cover ensures that the ball doesn't slip, adding a little stability to make the ball less tippy for sitting.

FINISHED SIZE

24 in (61 cm) diameter

SKILL LEVEL

Intermediate

YARN

Bernat Maker Home Dec; #5 bulky-weight yarn; 72% cotton, 28% nylon; 317 yd (290 m), 8.8 oz (250 g) per skein; machine wash and dry

- **A:** 2 skeins #11012 Black
- **B:** 2 skeins #11009 Cream

You will need to divide the skeins evenly into 3 center-pull bobbins/balls.

NEEDLES

Size US 19 (15.0 mm) circular needle, 40 in (101.6 cm) long, or size to obtain gauge

NOTIONS

Tapestry needle
22 in (56 cm) diameter fitness ball

GAUGE

7.5 sts x 11 rows in stockinette stitch with three strands of yarn held tog = 4 in (10 cm) square

SPECIAL ABBREVIATIONS

PM: Place stitch marker.
SM: Slip stitch marker.

Pattern

Work holding three strands tog as one.

With **A** CO 42 sts. Join and work in the rnd.

Rnd 1: *K7, PM, rep from * to end of rnd. (42 sts)

Rnd 2: *Knit to last st before marker, kfb, SM, rep from * to end of rnd. (48 sts)

Rnd 3: Knit all sts, slipping the markers as you go.

Rnd 4: *Knit to last st before marker, kfb, SM, rep from * to end of rnd. (54 sts)

Change to color **B**.

Rnds 5–8: Rep rnds 3–4. (66 sts)

Change to color **A**.

Rnds 9–12: Rep rnds 3–4. (78 sts)

Change to color **B**.

Rnds 13–16: Rep rnds 3–4. (90 sts)

Change to color **A**.

Rnds 17–20: Rep rnds 3–4. (102 sts)

Change to color **B**.

Rnds 21–24: Rep rnds 3–4. (114 sts)

Change to color **A**.

Rnds 25–28: Knit all sts, slipping the markers as you go.

Change to color **B**.

Rnds 29–32: Knit all sts, slipping the markers as you go.

Change to color **A**.

Rnds 33–36: Knit all sts, slipping the markers as you go.

Change to color **B**.

Rnds 37–40: Knit all sts, slipping the markers as you go.

Change to color **A**.

Rnds 41–44: Knit all sts, slipping the markers as you go.

Change to color **B**.

Rnd 45: Knit all sts, slipping the markers as you go.

Rnd 46: *Knit to last 2 sts before marker, k2tog, SM, rep from * to end of rnd. (108 sts)

Rnd 47: Knit all sts, slipping the markers as you go.

Rnd 48: *Knit to last 2 sts before marker, k2tog, SM, rep from * to end of rnd. (102 sts)

Change to color **A**.

Rnds 49–52: Rep rnds 47–48. (90 sts)

Change to color **B**.

Rnds 53–56: Rep rnds 47–48. (78 sts)

Change to color **A**.

Rnds 57–60: Rep rnds 47–48. (66 sts)

Change to color **B**.

Rnds 61–64: Rep rnds 47–48. (54 sts)

Change to color **A**.

Rnds 65–68: Rep rnds 47–48. (42 sts)

Change to color **B**.

Rnds 69–72: Rep rnds 47–48. (30 sts)

Change to color **A**.

Rnds 73–76: Rep rnds 47–48. (18 sts)

Change to color **B**.

Rnd 77: *Knit to last 2 sts before marker, k2tog, remove marker, rep from * to end of rnd. (12 sts)

Rnd 78: K2tog to end of rnd. (6 sts)

Break yarn and weave through last 6 sts. Pull tight to cinch hole in top and tie off. Weave in loose ends.

Finishing

Stuff cover and inflate ball inside.

Hexagon Throw Blanket

Sweet dreams! This throw blanket is the perfect size for cuddling up with baby while rocking him to sleep. Apricot and navy intermingle with white in a pixelating hexagonal pattern that is the perfect combination of modern and cozy.

FINISHED SIZE
36 x 48 in (91 x 122 cm)

SKILL LEVEL
Advanced

YARN
Patons Astra; #3 light-weight yarn; 100% acrylic; 161 yd (147 m), 1.75 oz (50 g) per skein; machine wash and dry
- **A:** 14 skeins #012751 White
- **B:** 4 skeins #02731 Apricot
- **C:** 3 skeins #02849 Navy

You will need three strands at 3½ yd (3.2 m) each for each color square on the colorwork chart.

NEEDLES
Size US 15 (10.0 mm) circular needle, 40 in (102 cm) long, or size to obtain gauge

NOTIONS
Tapestry needle

GAUGE
12 sts x 16 rows in pattern stitch with three strands held tog = 4 in (10 cm) square

Pattern

Work holding three strands tog as one.

With **A** CO 100 sts.

Follow the color chart on pages 84–85 while working the rows as follows:

Row 1 (RS): Knit all sts.

Row 2 (WS): Knit all sts.

Row 3: K2, *with yarn at WS sl 1 st pwise, k6, with yarn at WS sl 1 st pwise, rep from * to last 2 sts, k2.

Row 4: K2, *with yarn at WS sl 1 st pwise, p6, with yarn at WS sl 1 st pwise, rep from * to last 2 sts, k2.

Rows 5–8: Rep rows 3–4.

Rows 9–12: Knit all sts.

Row 13: K5, with yarn at WS sl 1 st pwise, *with yarn at WS sl 1 st pwise, k6, with yarn at WS sl 1 st pwise, rep from * to last st 6 sts, with yarn at WS, sl 1 st pwise, k5.

Row 14: K2, p3, with yarn at WS sl 1 st pwise, *with yarn at WS sl 1 st pwise, p6, with yarn at WS sl 1 st pwise, rep from * to last 6 sts, with yarn at WS sl 1 st pwise, p3, k2.

Rows 15–18: Rep rows 3–4.

Rows 19–20: Knit all sts.

Rows 21–220: Rep rows 1–20 while following the color chart.

Rows 221–230: Rep rows 1–10 while following the color chart.

BO all sts. Break yarn.

Finishing

Weave in ends.

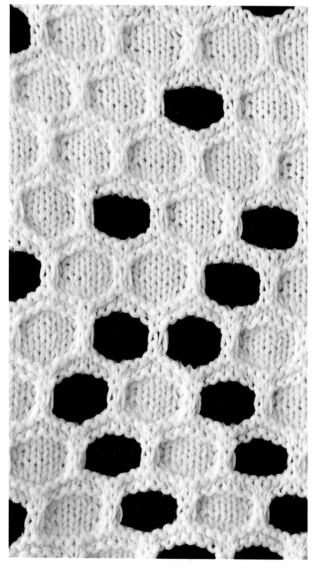

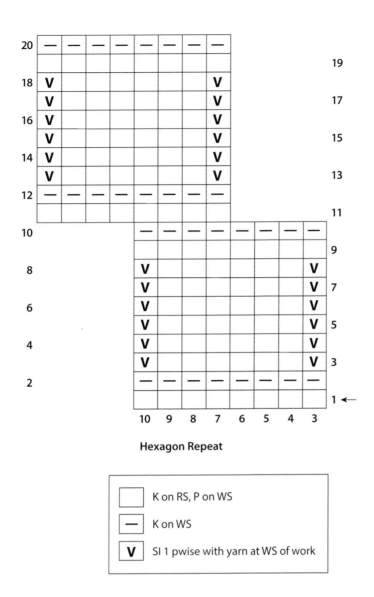

Hexagon Repeat

	K on RS, P on WS
—	K on WS
V	Sl 1 pwise with yarn at WS of work

Key for chart on pages 84–85

	K on RS, P on WS
—	K on WS
V	Sl 1 pwise with yarn at WS of work

Color

	Yarn A
	Yarn B
	Yarn C

229 227 225 223 221 219 217 215 213 211 209 207 205 203 201 199 197 195 193 191 189 187 185 183 181 179 177 175 173 171 169 167 165 163 161 159 157 155 153 151 149 147 145 143 141 139 137 135 133 131 129 127 125 123 121 119 117 115

230 228 226 224 222 220 218 216 214 212 210 208 206 204 202 200 198 196 194 192 190 188 186 184 182 180 178 176 174 172 170 168 166 164 162 160 158 156 154 152 150 148 146 144 142 140 138 136 134 132 130 128 126 124 122 120 118 116 114

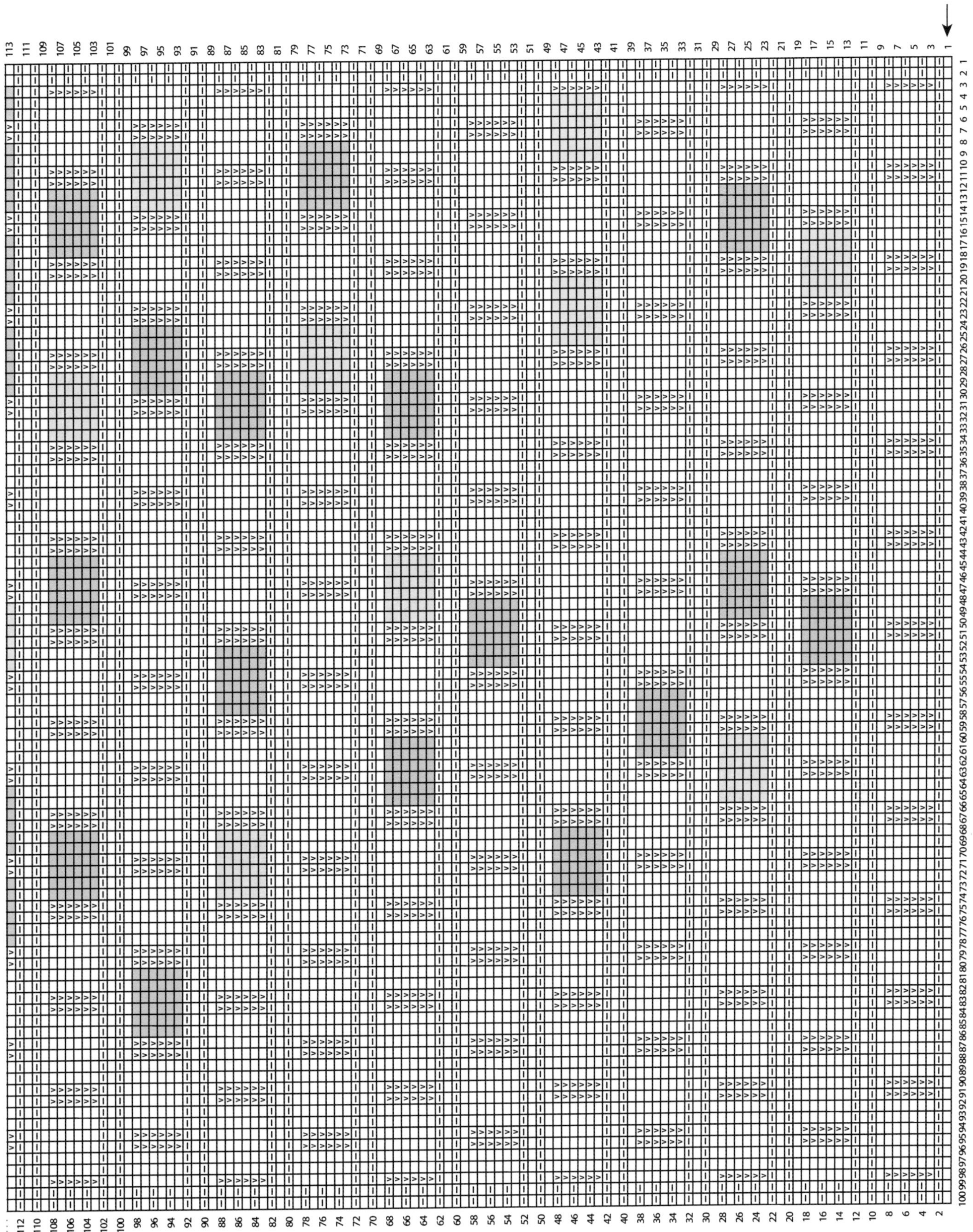

Triangle Baby Blanket

Baby, baby! Bright colors and triangles make up the pattern for this adorable, modern baby blanket. The triple-thick yarn makes this blanket cushiony soft and the perfect throw to keep baby safe while she explores on the floor during tummy time.

FINISHED SIZE
39 x 37 in (99 x 94 cm)

SKILL LEVEL
Advanced

YARN
Caron Simply Soft; #4 medium-weight yarn; 100% acrylic; 315 yd (288 m), 6 oz (170 g) per skein; machine wash and dry
- **A:** 1 skein #9772 Neon Coral

Bernat Super Value; #4 medium-weight yarn; 100% acrylic; 426 yd (389 m), 7 oz (197 g) per skein; machine wash and dry
- **B:** 2 skeins #08886 Mint
- **C:** 2 skeins #07407 Winter White

Required Bobbins:
*One three-stranded bobbin of 15 yd (14 m) for each trian-gle (3 **A**, 29 **B**, 31 **C**)*

*One three-stranded bobbin of 5 yd (4.5 m) for each partial triangle (6 **B**, 8 **C**)*
*One three-stranded bobbin of 25 yd (23 m) in **A** for the left side of the trim in the main body of the blanket.*

NEEDLES
Size US 15 (10.0 mm) circular needle, 40 in (101.6 cm) long, or size to obtain gauge

NOTIONS
Tapestry needle

GAUGE
9 sts x 13 rows in stockinette stitch with three strands of yarn held tog = 4 in (10 cm) square

Pattern

Work holding three strands tog as one.
With **A** CO 85 sts.
Follow the color chart while working as follows:
Rows 1–4: Knit all sts.
Row 5: Knit all sts.
Row 6: K3, p to last 3 sts, k3.
Rows 7–116: Rep rows 5–6.
Rows 117–120: Knit all sts.
BO all sts. Break yarn.

Finishing

Weave in ends.

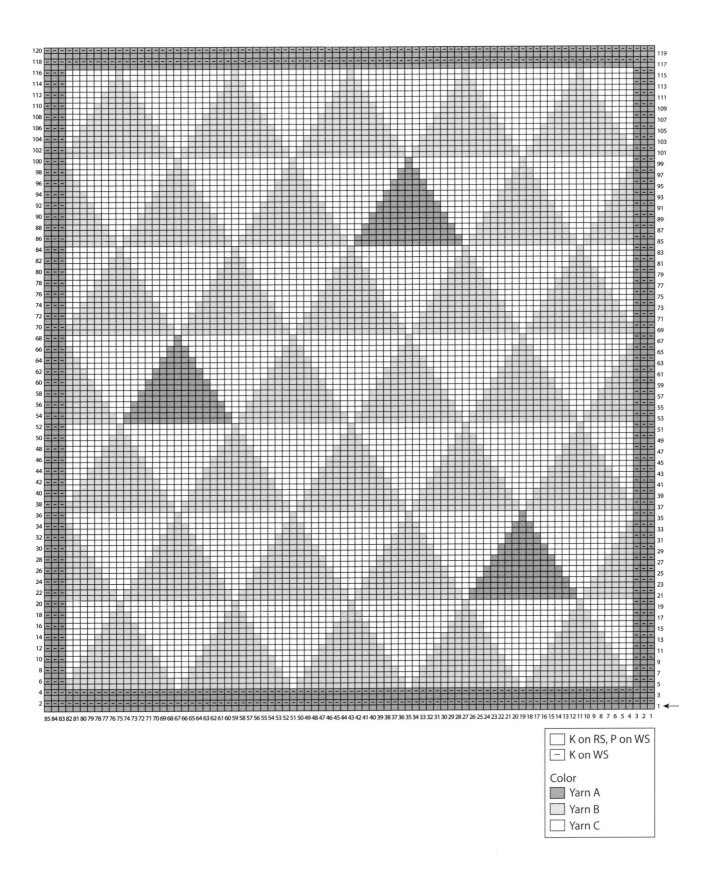

Textural Lovie

Textures abound in this truly unique lovie. The small, portable size and the entertaining textures ensure that this will be a well-loved cuddly soother. The best part is that the quality of this piece makes it a gorgeous work of art that could easily become the centerpiece of the nursery.

FINISHED SIZE
12 x 13 in (30 x 33 cm), plus fringe

SKILL LEVEL
Intermediate

YARN
Caron Simply Soft; #4 medium-weight yarn; 100% acrylic; 315 yd (288 m), 6 oz (170 g) per skein; machine wash and dry
- **A:** 1 skein #9772 Neon Coral

Bernat Super Value; #4 medium-weight yarn; 100% acrylic; 426 yd (389 m), 7 oz (197 g) per skein; machine wash and dry
- **B:** 1 skein #07407 Winter White
- **C:** 1 skein #08886 Mint

Patons Astra; #3 light-weight yarn; 100% acrylic; 161 yd (147 m), 1.75 oz (50 g) per skein; machine wash and dry
- **D:** 1 skein #02849 Navy
- **E:** 1 skein #02731 Apricot

Required Bobbins:
*In yarn **A** wind one three-stranded bobbin of 25 yd (23 m) for bottom, right, and top trim; one three-stranded bobbin of 8 yd (7.5 m) for left trim; one three-stranded bobbin of 6 yd (5.5 m) for middle stripe.*
*In yarn **B** wind one three-stranded bobbin of 15 yd (14 m) for right side; one three-stranded bobbin of 22 yd (20 m) for left side.*
*In yarn **C** wind one three-stranded bobbin of 15 yd (14 m) for triangle.*
*In yarn **D** wind one three-stranded bobbin of 18 yd (16.5 m) for bobbles.*
*In yarn **E** wind one three-stranded bobbin of 13 yd (12 m) for bobbles.*

NEEDLES
Size US 15 (10.0 mm) needles, 14 in (36 cm) long, or size to obtain gauge
US N/P (10.0 mm) crochet hook, for attaching fringe

NOTIONS
Tapestry needle

GAUGE
8 sts x 14 rows in stockinette stitch with three strands of yarn held tog = 4 in (10 cm) square

SPECIAL TECHNIQUES
Fringe on page 116
Pom-poms on page 115

SPECIAL ABBREVIATIONS

Bobble: In same st (k1, yo, k1, yo, k1), turn, purl all 5 sts from bobble, turn, knit all 5 sts from bobble, turn, purl all 5 sts from bobble, turn, k5tog.

Pattern

Work holding three strands tog as one.
With **A** CO 28 sts.
Follow the color chart while you work as follows:
Rows 1–4: Knit all sts.
Row 5: Knit all sts.
Row 6: K3, purl to last 3 sts, k3.
Rows 7–12: Rep rows 5–6.
Row 13: Knit all sts.
Row 14: K3, p15, k1, p6, k3.
Row 15: K7, bobble, knit to end of row.
Row 16: K3, p14, k2, p6, k3.
Row 17: K22, bobble, knit to end of row.
Row 18: K3, p13, k3, p6, k3.
Row 19: Knit all sts.
Row 20: Rep row 18.
Row 21: K8, bobble, k10, bobble, knit to end of row.
Row 22: Rep row 18.
Row 23: Knit all sts.
Row 24: Rep row 18.
Row 25: K4, bobble, k8, bobble, knit to end of row.
Row 26: Rep row 18.
Row 27: K22, bobble, knit to end of row.
Row 28: Rep row 18.
Row 29: Knit all sts
Row 30: Rep row 18.
Row 31: K17, bobble, knit to end of row.
Row 32: Rep row 18.
Row 33: K5, bobble, knit to end of row.
Row 34: Rep row 18.
Row 35: K14, bobble, knit to end of row.
Row 36: Rep row 18.
Row 37: K7, bobble, k14, bobble, knit to end of row.
Row 38: Rep row 18.
Row 39: Knit all sts.
Row 40: Rep row 18.
Rows 41–44: Knit.
BO all sts. Break yarn. Weave in loose ends.

Finishing

Using three 13 in (33 cm) strands of yarn **C** per fringe section, attach fringe through each stitch along the bottom of the triangle.

Using three 13 in (33 cm) strands of yarn **B** per fringe section, attach fringe through each stitch along the CO.

Using yarn **A** make one 4 in (10 cm) diameter pom-pom. Tie the pom-pom to the corner of the lovie by weaving one 14 in (35.56 cm) strand of yarn **A** through the center of the pom-pom and through the corner of the blanket. Secure by tying a tight bow that will keep the pom-pom secure but will allow it to be removed before washing your lovie.

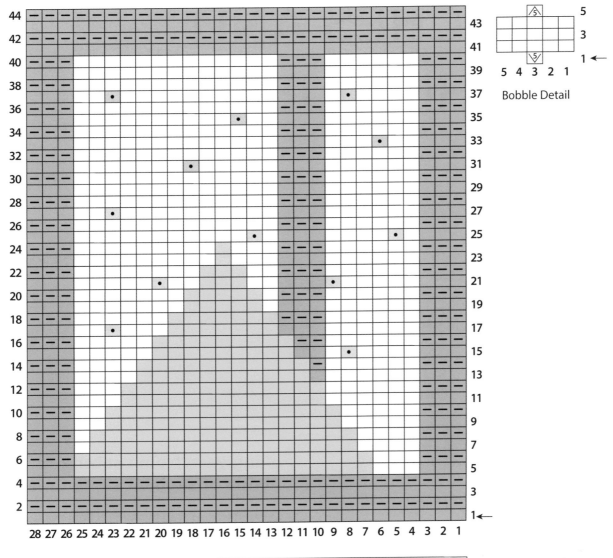

Bobble Detail

	K on RS, P on WS
−	K on WS
•	**Bobble in same st** (K1, yo, k1, yo, k1), turn, p all 5 sts from bobble, turn, k all 5 sts from bobble, turn, p all 5 sts from bobble, turn, k5tog
⑤	K1, yo, k1, yo, k1
⑤	K5tog

Color

| | Yarn A | | Yarn C | | Yarn E |
| | Yarn B | | Yarn D | | |

STITCHES AND TECHNIQUES

Knitting with Multiple Strands

Sometimes the number of skeins called for won't be easily divisible by the number of strands you will need to use for the pattern. In this instance you can either increase the number of skeins to be divisible evenly by the number of strands, knowing that you will end up with leftover yarn, or you can break down the skeins into smaller balls.

The easiest way to break down a skein is to decide how many balls you want to make from your single skein, weigh the skein, divide the weight by the number of skeins you want, and then portion out each mass of yarn to form the new balls.

Pulling yarn from center of skein

Pulling the yarn from the center of the skein will keep your skein in place as you work. Simply reach your fingers into the hole in the center of the skein and pull out some yarn. With any luck you will be able to find the end right away, although sometimes you do wind up with a few yarn guts being spilled.

Pulling yarn from center and outside of skein at same time

If you want to work with two strands from the same skein, just pull the end from the center of the skein and pull the end from the outside of the skein and hold them together as one strand. Although your skein will dance around as you work from it, the two strands don't tend to tangle with each other.

Center-pull bobbin

When you have to break down skeins of yarn into smaller portions to use multiple strands, or for doing colorwork, winding a center-pull bobbin is a great way to keep your yarn organized. To wind a bobbin:

1. Take the end of your yarn and secure it against your palm with your pinky finger.

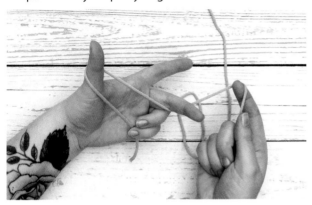

2. Wind the working end of your yarn in a figure-eight pattern between your thumb and pointer finger.

3. Continue winding until most of your yarn has been used.

4. Remove the yarn from your fingers and secure the bobbin by wrapping your remaining length of yarn around the center.

5. You can now pull your working yarn from the wound section of the bobbin.

Center-pull ball

You may end up with larger amounts of yarn than can be comfortably wound into a bobbin. In these instances you may want to use the center-pull ball technique. To wind a center-pull ball:

1. Create a center-pull bobbin with the first few yards of your yarn.

2. Continue wrapping your yarn around the bobbin until you get a tubular shape.

3. Start winding your yarn the long way around your tube, working from the bottom left side of the tube, up and over the top right side of the tube, turning the tube a quarter turn with every wrap. (Ensure that the end of yarn hanging from the bobbin remains loose and doesn't get covered up.)

4. As you continue you will start to see the ball take shape.

5. You now have a center-pull pineapple (isn't it cute?). You can tuck the end of the yarn under a wrap to secure and pull your working yarn from the center of the ball, or you can pull from both the center and outside of the ball for two strands.

Casting On

Slipknot

A slipknot is the first loop you will make on your needle, and it counts as the first cast-on stitch. To make a slipknot:

1. Make a loop about 8 in (20 cm) from the end of your yarn.

2. With your working yarn, make another loop and pull it through the center of the first loop.

3. Pull the second loop and your yarn tail to tighten the base of the slipknot.

4. Place the loop over your needle and pull your working yarn to tighten the loop.

Crochet Cast-on

Although this isn't the most basic cast-on, it is my preferred method as it creates a cast-on edge that almost perfectly matches a basic bind-off edge. When you are working with large gauge stitches, the edges are more visible, so this will have an impact on your finished project.

1. Make a slipknot and place the loop on your RH needle (or a crochet hook of the same gauge that can help you grab the loops more easily), and place your LH needle alongside, parallel to your first needle.

2. Wrap your working yarn behind and around the front of your LH needle, passing across the front of the RH needle.

3. Use the tip of your RH needle to draw the yarn through the loop and onto your needle. You now have one stitch on your LH needle and one stitch on your RH needle.

4. Continue steps 2 and 3, adding a stitch to your LH needle with each pass until you have one stitch less on your LH needle than your pattern calls for.

5. Slip the stitch from your RH needle onto your LH needle to finish the cast-on.

Knitted Cast-on

This is probably the easiest cast-on method for a beginner to use because it uses the same principles and techniques as the actual knit stitch. It is also the perfect cast-on method for casting on stitches in the middle of a row.

1. Make a slipknot and place the loop on your LH needle.

2. Insert your needle into the first stitch knitwise and wrap your working yarn around the back of the needle and across the front as if to knit.

3. Draw the yarn through the stitch and up onto your needle to form a loop.

4. Place the loop onto the LH needle. You now have 2 stitches on your LH needle.

5. Continue repeating steps 2 through 5 until you have the correct number of stitches on your LH needle.

Casting-on in the Round for Circular Needles

Use your preferred cast-on-method to cast stitches onto your circular needles. When you have the appropriate number of stitches, you will need to join your work in the round.

1. Cast on one extra stitch. Spread your stitches evenly across the circular needle. Place your working needle (needle that holds the stitch with your working yarn attached to it) and your working yarn in your right hand and the other needle in your left hand. Make sure that your stitches aren't twisted.

2. Slip the first stitch (your extra stitch) to your LH needle.

3. Work your first two stitches together as one stitch.

4. Continue working around.

Turkish Cast-on

This cast-on method allows you to cast on stitches to begin knitting in the round while creating a closed end, perfect for a toe-up sock. You will need to use a 36 in (91 cm) or longer circular needle for this method.

1. Place your needles side by side, running parallel to each other, with the tips pointing in the same direction. Make a slipknot and place it on the front needle.

2. Wrap your yarn from the bottom over the tip and back around both needles (each wrap creates two stitches).

3. Continue wrapping in this manner until you have one less than your required number of stitches. Bring your yarn over the back needle and drop it between your two needles.

4. Use the magic loop method (see next tutorial) to knit your first round to complete this cast-on.

Magic Loop

The magic loop method is a great alternative to using double-pointed needles to knit small circumferences in the round (like socks).

1. Using your preferred method, cast your stitches onto a long circular needle in the size designated in your pattern. Evenly divide your stitches into two groups with one group on one needle tip and one group on the other needle tip. Place your needles side by side, running parallel to each other, with the tips pointing in the same direction. Make sure your working needle (needle that holds the stitch with your working yarn attached to it) is at the back.

2. Slip the back needle out, pulling the cord through the stitches, and work the front stitches.

3. Pull your empty needle back so that the stitches that were sitting on the cord are now on your empty needle.

4. Turn your work.

5. Repeat steps 2 through 4 to continue working in the round.

Stitches

Knitting Flat versus Knitting in the Round

When knitting right-handed in the English style, you will hold the needle holding your stitches in your left hand and your working needle and your working yarn in your right hand. Your working needle (right-hand needle) will be used to create each new stitch. You can use either straight needles or circular needles to knit flat; when you reach the end of a row, you will simply turn your work and switch hands to start the process again for the next row. To knit in the round, you can use a circular needle or double-pointed needles. When you reach the end of a round, you will simply continue knitting in the same direction as you slide your stitches around your circular needle or double-pointed needles.

Knit Stitch

The knit stitch is the most basic stitch in a knitter's arsenal.

1. With your working yarn to the back of your work, insert your right-hand needle up into the first stitch on your left-hand needle. Wrap your working yarn around the back and across the front of the tip of your right-hand needle.

2. Draw the yarn through the stitch to form a loop on your right-hand needle.

3. Slide the stitch off of your left-hand needle.

4. Continue in this manner to knit each stitch.

Purl Stitch

The purl stitch is the second stitch you will need to know.

1. With your working yarn to the front of your work, insert your right-hand needle down into the first stitch on your left-hand needle. Wrap your working yarn over the top and up under the bottom of the tip of your right-hand needle.

2. Draw the yarn through the stitch to form a loop on your right-hand needle.

3. Slide the stitch off of your left-hand needle.

4. Continue in this manner to purl each stitch.

The knit and purl stitches are the two stitches you will use for knitting. Once you have mastered these, you should be able to work most stitches, and it is time to tackle some more advanced techniques.

Decreases

K2TOG (knit two together)

The k2tog is a right-slanting decrease (when worked on the right side of the work) created by simply knitting two stitches together as a single stitch. This same technique can be used to decrease by any number of stitches by simply knitting the stitches together as one.

P2TOG (purl two together)

The p2tog is the wrong-side equivalent of the k2tog and generally is worked on the wrong side of the work to create a right-slanting decrease on the right side of the work. As with the k2tog, this technique can be used to decrease by any number of stitches.

SSK (slip, slip, knit)

The ssk is a left-slanting decrease (when worked on the right side of the work).

1. Slip one stitch knitwise to the right-hand needle.

2. Slip one stitch purlwise to the right-hand needle.

3. Place tip of the left-hand needle through the front of both slipped stitches and knit them both together.

K2TOG TBL (knit two together through the back loop)
The k2tog tbl is a left-slanting decrease (when worked on the right side of the work) and is created by simply knitting two stitches together through the back legs of the stitches.

Increases

KFB (knit through the front and back of the stitch)
The kfb is used to increase by one stitch. You can increase by a larger number of stitches by using the same technique and alternately knitting through the front and back of a stitch (i.e., kfbf will increase by 2 stitches, kfbfb will increase by 3 stitches, kfbfbf will increase by 4 stitches, etc.).

1. Knit through the front loop, but don't slide the stitch off the needle.

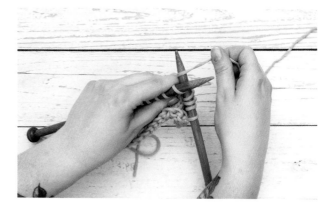

2. Knit through the back loop before sliding the stitch off the needle.

YO (yarn over)
The yo is used to increase by one stitch or to create holes in lacy fabrics. It's really as easy as it sounds: Simply bring your working yarn to the front of your work and then continue knitting. This creates an extra stitch on your needle where the yarn was wrapped.

Cable Stitches

Knitting cables can be intimidating for a lot of people, but it really isn't as hard as it may seem. To start, you will need a cable needle. There are a few varieties out there, but it is really just a question of personal preference. I tend to use a standard double-pointed needle because I always have them on hand. It is probably best practice to use a cable needle that is the same gauge as the needles you are using for your project, but in reality the needles are simply a means to hold stitches and move them from one place to another, so I never have worried about it; I just used my handy US 8 (5.0 mm) double-pointed needle.

Cables are created by working stitches out of order so that some cross over others. The same technique is used when creating cables with any number of stitches. I will show you examples of just C6F and C6B, but the technique is the same for all of the cables in this book. The "6" in the abbreviation means that you will be working with six stitches, divided in half so that three will go either in front ("F") or back ("B") of the other three stitches.

C6F (cable 6 front)

1. Slip the next 3 stitches to cable needle and hold in front of work.

2. Knit 3 from left-hand needle.

3. Knit 3 from cable needle.

4. You have completed one twist of your cable.

C6B (cable 6 back)

The C6B is worked the same as the C6F, except you hold the stitches in the back instead of the front while you work the cable.

Color Changes

Intarsia

Intarsia is a technique where you work blocks of color within a piece using separate skeins of yarn for each block of color in your pattern. When knitting intarsia you will need to twist your yarns at each color change to prevent holes from appearing in your work. When working on a vertical color change you will twist your yarn on every row, while when working on a diagonal color change, you will only have to twist your yarn on every other row.

1. To twist the colors, insert your needle into the first stitch that will be the new color and lay the old yarn color over the needle.

2. Work the stitch in the new color, dropping the old color as you slide the stitch off of your needle.

Binding Off

Basic Bind-off

This is the most commonly used bind-off and will create a neat and tidy chain along the bind-off edge of your work. Be sure to bind off loosely enough that there is some give to your edge. Some people prefer to bind off with a needle one size larger than what they used to knit the piece to ensure a loose enough bind-off.

1. Knit the first stitch from your left-hand needle.

2. Knit the next stitch from your left-hand needle.

3. Insert the tip of your left-hand needle into the second stitch on your right-hand needle.

4. Pass this stitch over the first stitch and off the needle (there is now only one stitch on your right-hand needle).

5. Repeat steps 2 through 4 until only one stitch remains. Break your yarn and draw it through the final stitch and secure.

Purl Bind-off

The purl bind-off is worked in the same manner as the basic bind-off, but instead of knitting the stitches you purl them.

Finishing

Seaming

There are a million ways to seam pieces of knitting together. Here are a few used in this book:

MATTRESS STITCH (Invisible Vertical Seam)
This technique creates an invisible seam on stockinette stitch fabric.

1. Place pieces to be seamed side by side with the right side facing you. With a yarn needle and matching piece of yarn, insert the needle under the first bar on the edge of one piece of fabric.

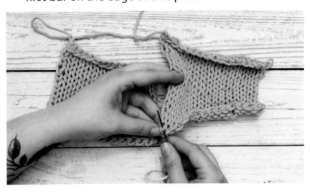

2. Insert the needle under the first bar on the edge of the other piece of fabric.

3. Continue in this manner, weaving back and forth under each bar, until the entire seam has been stitched together.

4. Be sure to pull the yarn taut to fully close the seam.

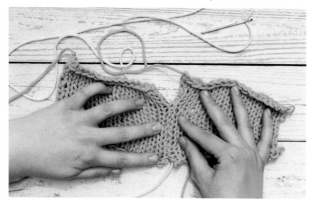

INVISIBLE HORIZONTAL SEAM

This technique creates an invisible seam on stockinette stitch by mimicking a row of knit stitches.

1. Place pieces to be seamed end to end with the right side facing you. With a yarn needle and matching piece of yarn, insert the needle up through the center of the first stitch on the bottom piece.

2. Insert the needle under both legs of the first stitch on the top piece.

3. Insert the needle back down through the center of the first stitch on the bottom piece.

4. Continue in this manner, weaving up, under, and back down, through each stitch until the entire seam has been stitched together.

CROCHET SLIP STITCH TOGETHER

This technique creates a sturdy seam that can be worked on the wrong side or the right side of the fabric. When worked on the right side, the stitch creates a beautiful accent chain similar to a surface slip stitch.

1. Place the pieces to be seamed one on top of the other, either right-side to right-side for a hidden seam or wrong-side to wrong-side for a visible accent seam, and insert the crochet hook through the same stitch on both pieces.

2. Wrap the yarn around the hook and draw a loop through the fabric and onto the hook, leaving a tail that can be woven in later.

3. Insert the crochet hook through the next stitches on both pieces.

4. Wrap the yarn around the hook and draw through the loop on the hook.

5. Continue in this manner, inserting the hook through each stitch and drawing the yarn up through the fabric and through the loop on the hook until the entire seam has been stitched together.

WHIPSTITCH

The whipstich is the most simple form of seaming.

1. Place pieces to be seamed right side to right side together. With a yarn needle and matching piece of yarn, insert the needle through both pieces from back to front.

2. Continue in this manner, inserting the needle from back to front across the entire seam until it has been stitched together.

BACKSTITCH

This is my go-to seam for installing zippers—just be sure that you don't pull your stitches too taut, or you may end up with a puckered seam.

1. Place pieces to be seamed on top of each other, either right-side to right-side for a hidden seam or wrong-side to wrong-side for a visible accent seam. With a yarn needle and matching piece of yarn, insert the needle through both pieces from front to back.

2. Insert the needle through both pieces from back to front, over slightly from where you came through previously.

3. Insert the needle through both pieces from front to back through the hole created by your last front to back stitch.

4. Continue in this manner coming up through the back of the piece and going down through the front of the piece through the end of your previous stitch until the entire seam is stitched together.

KITCHENER STITCH

Kitchener stitch is used to graft live knit stitches together. The first two steps are different from the rest, but steps 4 through 8 repeat the pattern "kwise, pwise, pwise, kwise," and remembering this pattern can make the Kitchener stitch a little easier to follow.

1. Hold two live stitch edges side by side parallel to each other.

2. Insert the yarn needle with matching thread purlwise into the first stitch on the front needle and draw the yarn through.

3. Insert the needle knitwise into the first stitch on the back needle and draw the yarn through.

4. Insert the needle knitwise into the first stitch on the front needle, draw the yarn through, and slip the stitch off the needle.

5. Insert the needle purlwise into the next stitch on the front needle and draw the yarn through.

6. Insert the needle purlwise into the first stitch on the back needle, draw the yarn through, and slip the stitch off the needle.

7. Insert the needle knitwise into the next stitch on the back needle and draw the yarn through.

8. Continue repeating steps 4 through 7 until all of the stitches have been seamed together.

JOIN-AS-YOU-KNIT VERTICAL STRIPES

This joining method allows you to knit pieces that run parallel together and join them as you go.

1. Slip the first stitch on all right side rows.

2. Work the row until the last stitch and slip the last stitch onto your right-hand needle.

3. Slip your right-hand needle through the front leg of the first stitch of the corresponding row of the previous panel.

4. Place your left-hand needle through the front of the first two stitches on your right-hand needle and work both stitches together.

5. Turn your work and work the next row.

Zippers

Zippers add a finished touch to your knitted pillowcases while also making them removable and easy to care for. To install a zipper:

1. Center the closed zipper in the seam. (I like to sew the seam closed about 1 in [2.5 cm] on either end to make the zipper easier to install.)

2. Pin the zipper in place along multiple points on each side of the seam. Make sure to keep the teeth of the zipper away from the edges of your fabric to avoid snags.

3. Open the zipper. Sew each side of the zipper in place using a backstitch seam, in corresponding yarn, running just inside the edge of your knit fabric. I run my backstitching directly under the rolled lip on the cast-on or bind-off edge to ensure that it stays hidden.

Weaving in Ends

When you have completed your project, you will need to finish it by weaving in all of your ends. Use a yarn needle to weave all of your tails back and forth through the stitches on the wrong side of your work to secure them in place. For less noticeable ends, you can weave them in the same direction as the stitches (similar to the duplicate stitch technique) or weave them into a seam. When working with larger yarns and multiple strands, it may become necessary to secure the tails further to ensure that they don't come loose. In this instance you will want to use a needle and thread in a color that matches your yarn to whipstitch all of your ends in place.

Surface Slip Stitch

Surface slip stitch allows you to add color and detail to your pieces after they are finished. The chain created by this technique looks similar to the Vs of the stockinette stitch.

1. Insert the end of your hook into the first stitch along the edge of your piece and pull up a loop in your contrasting color. (Leave a tail that can be woven in later.)

2. Insert your hook into the next stitch.

3. Draw the yarn through and onto your hook.

4. Draw the loop through the loop on your hook.

5. Continue in this manner, inserting your hook into each stitch, wrapping the yarn, and drawing the yarn through the loop and onto your hook until you reach the opposite edge of your piece.

6. Break yarn and draw through remaining loop on hook and pull tight to secure.

Duplicate Stitch

The duplicate stitch is another form of surface decoration that can be added to your knitting once it has been finished. You will duplicate the stitches with a needle and yarn, essentially tracing your stitches to add color and texture to your project.

1. Using a needle and yarn in a contrasting color, insert the needle from the back to the front through the center bottom of the stitch to be worked.

2. Insert the needle under the two legs of the stitch above.

3. Insert the needle from the front to the back, back through the center bottom of the stitch.

4. Continue in this manner for each stitch.

Blocking

When you have finished your project, you will want to make it perfect by giving it a good soak and block. Start by soaking and washing your piece in lukewarm water (not too hot) with a gentle detergent. Once your piece has been thoroughly soaked, rinse out all of the detergent and gently press out as much water as you can. (You can sandwich your piece between a couple of thick colorfast towels and gently press out a lot of the moisture.) Finish by laying the piece flat and gently shaping it to the finished dimensions, smoothing out the stitches and straightening the edges as you go. Blocking has the most impact on natural fibers like wool, but I have also found it to be beneficial for acrylic pieces because it cleans the fabric and relaxes the stitches, making for a fantastic end result.

Finishing Touches

Finishing touches add the final polish to your projects. Whether you want fun and whimsical or elegant and classy, pom-poms, tassels, and fringe offer huge impact with minimal effort!

POM-POMS

1. Wrap your yarn many (many) times around a rectangular form (you can use your flat hand, a book, a piece of cardboard cut to size, whatever you have on hand).

2. Remove the yarn bundle from the form and tie a long piece of yarn securely around the middle a couple of times.

3. To add extra strength to the pom-pom, especially when you are making extraordinarily large pom-poms, take a yarn needle and weave the ends of your long piece of yarn through the center of the pom-pom a number of times to secure the strands in place. (You may also want to use a needle and thread to further secure your pom-pom strands.)

4. Cut the loops at both ends of the pom-pom.

5. Trim the pom-pom into shape.

TASSELS

1. Wrap your yarn a number of times around your fingers or a rectangular form.

2. Tie a long piece of yarn through the top of the yarn bundle.

3. Remove the yarn bundle from the form and tie another long piece of yarn around the needle just below the top. You can also wrap the yarn around the bundle a few times for added style, or add another tie for a different look.

4. Cut the loops at the bottom of the tassel.

5. Trim the yarn to shape the tassel and hide any long ends.

STRAIGHT FRINGE

1. Cut strands of yarn all the same length.

2. Insert crochet hook through stitch. Fold one strand of yarn in half to form a loop and draw the yarn loop back through the stitch.

3. Draw the ends of the strand through the loop and pull tight to secure.

4. Continue in this manner until your fringe is complete. (You can use multiple strands at a time to achieve a fuller fringe.)

LOOP FRINGE

1. Working on right side of piece with yarn needle threaded with a piece of yarn, insert needle through first stitch along seam and draw yarn through to end, leaving a tail. Insert needle through first stitch again and draw yarn through, leaving a 1½ in (4 cm) loop.

2. Secure the loop in place by knotting the yarn around the base of the loop.

3. Continue in this manner, inserting needle in next stitch, making a loop, and securing the loop, to form a loopy fringe around the perimeter of your piece. (Attach new strands of yarn as necessary and tie off and trim tails to finish the piece.)

Abbreviations

Approx	approximately
BO	bind off
C4B	cable four back: sl the next 2 sts to cn and hold at back of work, k2 from LH needle, k2 from cn
C4F	cable four front: sl the next 2 sts to cn and hold in front of work, k2 from LH needle, k2 from cn
C6B	cable six back: sl the next 3 sts to cn and hold in back of work, k3 from LH needle, k3 from cn
C6F	cable six front: sl the next 3 sts to cn and hold in front of work, k3 from LH needle, k3 from cn
cn	cable needle
CO	cast on
k	knit
k2tog	knit 2 stitches together
k2tog tbl	knit 2 together through the back loops: insert your RH needle through the back loop of two sts pwise, knit both sts tog
k5tog	knit 5 stitches together
kfb	knit into front and back of stitch to increase by 1 stitch

kwise	knitwise
LH	left hand
p	purl
p3tog	purl 3 stitches together
PM	place stitch marker
P tbl	purl through the back loop
pwise	purlwise
rep	repeat
RH	right hand
rnd(s)	round(s)
RS	right side
sl	slip
SM	slip stitch marker
ssk	slip, slip, knit: sl 1 st kwise to RH needle, sl 1 st pwise to RH needle, place tip of LH needle through front of both slipped sts, k2tog
st(s)	stitch(es)
tog	together
WS	wrong side
yo	yarn over

Knitting Needle Sizes
for this Book

Metric (mm)	U.S.
10.0	15
15.0	19
20.0	36
25.0	50

Yarn Weight Chart for this Book

Light	Medium	Bulky	Super Bulky
DK, Light Worsted	Worsted, Afghan, Aran	Chunky, Craft, Rug	Super Bulky, Roving

Standard Yarn Weight System

Categories of yarn, gauge ranges, and recommended needle and hook sizes

Yarn Weight Symbol & Category Names	**0** LACE	**1** SUPER FINE	**2** FINE	**3** LIGHT	**4** MEDIUM	**5** BULKY	**6** SUPER BULKY	**7** JUMBO
Type of Yarns in Category	Fingering, 10-Count Crochet Thread	Sock, Fingering, Baby	Sport, Baby	DK, Light Worsted	Worsted, Afghan, Aran	Chunky, Craft, Rug	Bulky, Roving	Jumbo, Roving
Knit Gauge Range in Stockinette Stitch to 4 inches*	33–40 sts**	27–32 sts	23–26 sts	21–24 st	16–20 sts	12–15 sts	7–11 sts	6 sts and fewer
Recommended Needle in Metric Size Range	1.5–2.25 mm	2.25–3.25 mm	3.25–3.75 mm	3.75–4.5 mm	4.5–5.5 mm	5.5–8 mm	8–12.75 mm	12.75 mm and larger
Recommended Needle in U.S. Size Range	000 to 1	1 to 3	3 to 5	5 to 7	7 to 9	9 to 11	11 to 17	17 and larger
Crochet Gauge Ranges in Single Crochet to 4 inches*	32–42 double crochets**	21–32 sts	16–20 sts	12–17 sts	11–14 sts	8–11 sts	7–9 sts	6 sts and fewer
Recommended Hook in Metric Size Range	Steel*** 1.6–1.4 mm Regular hook 2.25 mm	2.25–3.5 mm	3.5–4.5 mm	4.5–5.5 mm	5.5–6.5 mm	6.5–9 mm	9–15 mm	15 mm and larger
Recommended Hook in U.S. Size Range	Steel 6, 7, 8*** Regular hook B–1	B–1 to E–4	E–4 to 7	7 to I–9	I–9 to K–10½	K–10½ to M–13	M–13 to Q	Q and larger

* GUIDELINES ONLY: The above reflect the most commonly used gauges and needle or hook sizes for specific yarn categories.

** Lace weight yarns are usually knitted or crocheted on larger needles and hooks to create lacy, openwork patterns. Accordingly, a gauge range is difficult to determine. Always follow the gauge stated in your pattern.

*** Steel crochet hooks are sized differently from regular hooks—the higher the number, the smaller the hook, which is the reverse of regular hook sizing.

Source: Craft Yarn Council of America's **www.YarnStandards.com**

Source: Craft Yarn Council's www.YarnStandards.com

Yarn Sources

All of the beautiful yarns in this book are available from Yarnspirations.com, official home of Bernat, Caron, Lily Sugar'n Cream, and Patons. My gratitude to Yarnspirations for the generous yarn support!

Yarns Used in this Book

Bernat Maker Home Dec, used for Cable Knit Footstool on page 13, Simple Stockinette Basket Bag on page 60, Stripy Ball Cover on page 75

Bernat Roving, used for Pinstripe Blanket on page 30, Linen Stitch Pillowcase on page 36, Cozy Slipper Socks on page 50

Bernat Satin, used for Diamond Lace Blanket on page 40, Daisy Pillowcase on page 44, Eyelet Throw Blanket on page 47

Bernat Softee Chunky, used for Cable Stripes Throw Blanket on page 2, Pinstripe Blanket on page 30, Simple Stockinette Cocoon Blanket on page 54, Simple Stockinette Cushion on page 57

Bernat Super Value, used for Triangle Baby Blanket on page 86, Textural Lovie on page 90

Caron Simply Soft, used for Chevron Blanket on page 66, Panda Throw Blanket on page 69, Polka Dot Pillowcase on page 72

Lily Sugar'n Cream, used for Terrarium Sling on page 25

Patons Astra, used for Hexagon Throw Blanket on page 80, Textural Lovie on page 90

Patons Canadiana, used for Herringbone Throw Blanket on page 33, Linen Stitch Pillowcase on page 36

Patons Classic Wool Worsted, used for Triple Cable Lapghan on page 6 , Twisted Cable Cushion on page 10, Honeycomb Cushion on page 22, Eyelet Throw Blanket on page 47

Patons Silk Bamboo, used for Dandelion Throw on page 18